SACRED CONNECTIONS HORSEMANSHIP

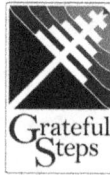

Grateful Steps Foundation
30 Ben Lippen School Road #107
Asheville, North Carolina 28806

Copyright © 2017 by Catherine Hunter

Library of Congress Control Number 2015908404
Hunter, Catherine
Sacred Connections Horsemanship
Empowering Horse and Rider through Chakra Energy

All photos are from the personal collection of Catherine Hunter unless otherwise specified in the caption. Cover picture of Marabeth Madsen on Dreamstar is photographed by Catherine Hunter.
The poem used in the dedication is an excerpt from
"A Trooper's Friend,"
by the late Sgt. Benjamin R. Gormley
Georgia Division Cavalry Reenactors
March 21, 1990.

ISBN 978-1-935130-80-2 Paperback

Printed in the United States of America
at Lightning Source

FIRST EDITION

www.gratefulsteps.org

For Count of War

If there be horses up in heaven . . .
May we ride together once again.

AUTHOR'S NOTE

I have had the good fortune of experiencing everything I ever dreamed of accomplishing with horses.

It is my great wish that others could also realize their dreams when it comes to horses and riding. Whether they dream of galloping through green fields, jumping high or winning in the big show, all riders should be able to do so without fear and without unconsciously hurting their faithful equine partners.

It is for that dream, that promise, these pages were written. I realized if I could do what I have done with horses—crossed sabers from the back of a great cavalry horse, charged with a lance, ridden across the country, galloped race horses, jumped high jumps and connected with my horse on such a deep level that we knew each other's most inner thoughts—others could reach their dreams and goals as well.

For me the answer was a system that was easy to understand, easy to implement and took into consideration my horse's thoughts, feelings and well-being. Though it may look like magic, deeply connecting with horses while riding is not.

Unfortunately, most riders today haven't had a clear system to follow. Though many have discovered a way to relate to, and enjoy their horses on the ground, they still dream of doing so while riding. Yet modern teaching techniques, geared for the show ring, often leave riders missing that deeper connection with their horses, or frustrated because they don't feel safe galloping through fields or over big jumps.

Within these pages the reader will discover a system that reaches back seven thousand years to the first horsemen on the Steppes of Asia. This system draws from the wisdom of the greatest horsemen throughout history and shows riders how to become bold and confident in the saddle and create loving, cooperative horses.

I encourage all riders to take heart. Don't stop dreaming. Follow the system. It will illuminate your way into enlightened, empowered partnership with your horse.

                                             - *Catherine Hunter*

Sacred Connections Horsemanship

Empowering Horse and Rider through Chakra Energy

Catherine Hunter

Grateful Steps
Asheville, North Carolina

Contents

Divine Equine

Together we have soared
Down secret trails and lanes;
Upon your wings I've dreamed
Of the hidden and arcane.

We've raced across green fields
And in fantasies I dream:
A magic sword I wield
Of light and brighter things.

I know silken touch,
Proud crest draped with mane
And ken wordless union
Through slightest breath of rein.

Together we have galloped
Past all my youthful fears,
For you blessed me with your silence
As I shed heartfelt tears.

I'll always hear the echo
Of your hooves upon the turf,
See sun dapple on your coat
As we shed the bonds of earth.

Together we will gallop
Down roads I'd ne'er have known.
For with my faithful horse
I'll never be alone.

– Catherine Hunter

Part I

Awakening the Mystery, Spirit and Magic

Chapter 1
Discovering the Mystique

Echoes of Count's hoofbeats bounced off empty windows in endless rows and rows of houses stacked against each other. Baltimore's drug dealers and prostitutes graced the street corners, and I couldn't see a blade of grass or a spot of green in the miles and miles of concrete and cracked pavement. I tried very hard not to be afraid.

"Le'me ride!" "I wanna ride!" called the children as they gathered around my horse. They played games of dare to see who was brave enough to come close to such a big animal, so foreign in their concrete world.

Then one young man named Sean, about 12 or 14 years old, looked me directly in the eye and said, "Teach me to ride."

I was dumbfounded. Of all the people I had met on my nine-hundred-mile ride to Ground Zero in New York City, I think the look in Sean's eyes affected me the most.

I could see that he *knew*. Sean had never been around horses, perhaps had never even seen one in real life, yet he knew. Sean saw the magic of horses. He saw the spirit, the hope and the dreams many of us see when we look at such magnificent creatures.

As I have so many times in my life, I began to wonder, what is it about horses? What makes us dream of riding? How is it we see such freedom, such spirit and such beauty in these beings and don't see it in others? Why do we not dream of riding cows, or elephants, or giraffes?

I know for myself, and I believe for many others, riding is a spiritual endeavor as much as, or perhaps more than, physical. Who among us has not dreamed of that butterfly-soft contact with a horse lightly dancing in response to our softest whisper of a command? Who has not yearned for that deep connection to the gods when galloping across a field or soaring over a four-foot wall?

The horse feels these things too. We see the horse's ears flop happily and his eyes become bright when he executes that perfect passage. We can feel the couple of soft bucks because the horse loves galloping across a green field, and we see his eagerness over a challenging jump course when the rider gives the horse his head and the freedom to be brilliant.

For generations the horse has captured the imagination of humans. It was the horse who won battles, and it was the horse the American Indians associated with both power and joy. Throughout history it was the person mounted on a horse who was noble.

I have come to wonder if the magic of horses is their immeasurable heart and spirit connecting us directly to the creative source. I believe it is this connection to the source of all creation that gives us a taste of the Sacred.

For thousands of years people have worked hard to ride correctly enough to make a true connection with their horses and taste that spirit of freedom and power the horse gives so generously. Yet riding correctly or riding well is not about how the rider looks in the saddle. It's not about whether her heels are down or her back is straight.

This true connection, this ability to ride far beyond correctness, happens when the horse shifts his energy from basic survival instincts and connects with the rider through trust. Once the horse begins to trust the rider, he is able to engage his mind over his instincts and connect with her on a pure energetic/spiritual level. The horse trusts the rider to treat him fairly, not to hurt or confuse him. The rider trusts the horse not to run away, buck her off, bolt or even stumble and fall.

Western cultures traditionally say trust—often described as an expression of love or friendship—resides in the heart. Eastern cultures observe this trust as an "energy pattern" of the heart "chakra."

> **Riding correctly is the physical manifestation of trust between horse and rider.**

Chakra is an ancient East Indian term used to describe the energy patterns connected to the body's systems, organs and emotional and spiritual structure. These patterns are located in the midline of the body (near the spine) and reflect both spiritual and physical energy. All creatures are considered to have seven chakras. The organization of these patterns functions similarly in both humans and animals. Chapters 2 and 3 contain more information about chakra energy patterns.

Until recent years, the term chakra was foreign to Western society. However, since the spiritual revolution of the 1960s, people in the Western world have become much more open to alternative approaches exploring spirituality and healing.

It is through the exploration and study of these energy patterns that Western theologians and healers are discovering the deep spiritual connections and alternative methods of healing that have been used in the Far East for thousands of years. For example, the ancient Chinese practice of Acupuncture, very common today in the United States, uses the body's energy patterns for amazing healing.

These energy patterns are recognized in varying ways throughout most cultures, though many use different terms. For example, Western culture uses a heart image to express love while Eastern Cultures talk about the energies of love and trust residing in the fourth, or heart chakra. Another example: the Chinese use the term "Chi energy" to describe personal power or courage, while people in the United States talk about "having the guts" to do something.

1. It is in the horse's and the rider's heart chakras that the energy of mutual trust resides.

Therefore it is in the horse's and the rider's heart chakras that the energy of mutual trust resides. Once the horse's heart chakra is open, it is possible to connect to the sacred energy in the horse's spirit and realize the promise of freedom we see when we gaze upon a horse.

If the rider works with the horse energetically, she can transform riding into a sacred experience. In order for the horse to be capable of an energetic or spiritual connection with his rider, he must shift from the physical concerns of survival to the energies of the mind and spirit.

Many riders dream of this type of riding, yet for most, the reality is far from the dream. Throughout the history of riding, masters of the sport have endeavored to pass on that esoteric relationship that transcends mere earthly bounds. Yet, until now this effort has encompassed years of hard work, often on a lunge line, sometimes accompanied with mantras such as, "heels down," "head up" or "up, down, up, down."

> **It is possible for the majority of today's riders to find that sacred connection with their horses.**

Historically, a deep spiritual relationship with horses was reserved for the most dedicated of horsemen or women who had the luxury of training for years to find a spark of that special connection. Others are left with reading about it in books or vicariously experiencing it through Hollywood's fantasies of horses.

However, it is possible for the majority of today's riders to find that sacred connection while riding. One does not have to become an expert horseman or woman to achieve that deep level of communication and understanding.

To achieve this level of communication, the rider must achieve the main goal of horsemanship, which is to bring the horse energetically up into his higher chakras and connect through the horse's fourth, fifth, sixth or seventh chakras. Clearing, opening and connecting with the horse's chakras is accomplished when the rider meets all of the horse's needs such as nutrition and safety, using communication he can understand, riding in a way that preserves his natural balance and movement, and protecting him from fear, pain and confusion. Though this is typically found in high levels of riding, even inexperienced riders can begin to attain this spiritual connection with their horses.

The energy of trust which lies in the fourth chakra is the key factor. By using simple, clear signals and a functional seat, inexperienced riders can establish trust with their horses and engage their horses' fourth chakra. The deeper and more continuous alignment the rider desires, the higher in the horse's chakras she must connect. A continuous sacred flow of energy between horse and rider is possible when the rider engages the horse's seventh chakra.

> **In order to make the sacred connection even briefly, the rider must bring the horse energetically up into his higher chakras.**

Many people have recently found a connection with the true spirit of horses from the ground by using various types of ground work to energetically interact with horses. As wonderful a relationship as this is, people want more. They want the same kind of relationship *while riding*.

If we work with the horse from the ground, allowing him complete freedom from restraint, the horse can relate to us purely from an energetic level. In certain types of ground work, we are, in essence, allowing the horse to open his chakras and be fully authentic. If the horse does not feel threatened or confined, we can share a pure, honest and complete exchange of energy.

If the rider can duplicate this freedom while mounted, the horse will be able to open his chakras and connect directly with her in the same manner. However, unlike ground work, riding brings in a new set of factors.

> The question arises as to why the relationship for most riders does not transfer from the ground to the saddle.

In order for the horse to open his chakras, he must be able to trust the rider. In order for the horse to trust the rider, she must first clear away the interference of her unconscious actions. A horse simply cannot relate to the rider on a meaningful level if he is trying to sort through a lot of unconscious chatter, conflicting signals or discomfort from the rider's seat, hands or legs.

In addition to riding in a way that does not distract the horse or interfere with his natural movement and natural response to signals, the rider must be able to clearly communicate her expectations. She must also develop in the horse the physical ability to perform required movements while maintaining the horse's spirit and desire to respond.

The horse may also have to contend with several physical factors that can affect his ability to fully open his chakras. For example if the saddle is pinching the horse's shoulder or the horse's back hurts because of poorly trimmed hooves, the horse will remain stuck in the survival energy of the first chakra. He simply cannot lift his concentration to higher levels when he is threatened by pain.

Until these basic physical factors are addressed, the horse may become stuck in whatever areas correspond to the physical factors affecting him. Therefore the rider must be certain the horse is healthy, has adequate nutrition and is sufficiently pain free to focus on training rather than his physical issues. Chapter 14 contains more information regarding hidden health and nutrition issues that can affect a horse's ability to connect more deeply with the rider.

In addition to his own physical concerns, the horse must also contend with the energies the rider adds when she sits on him. When mounted, the rider places her first and second chakras and all the energy of those areas directly on the horse's third and fourth chakras, which contain the energy patterns of self-confidence and trust. This transfers all the patterns the rider holds in her first and second chakras into the horse's self-confidence and heart energies.

For example, if the rider feels insecure, uncertain or afraid, she immediately transfers these feelings to the horse, affecting his self-confidence and ability to trust. The old saying, "A horse can sense the rider's fear," expresses this energy exchange between horse and rider.

In essence, just as people do, the horse manifests into the energetic what is happening to him on the physical plane. It is interesting to note that mules, who are known for demanding they be treated fairly, react very strongly to confusing or hurtful treatment. I have used Sacred Connections Horsemanship to retrain a couple of mules with great success. Since mules invariably respond to fair, just, consistent treatment that makes sense to them, this system can be used for mules with great results.

> **The horse manifests into the energetic what is happening to him on the physical plane.**

2. As shown here with stiff, hollow back, raised head and stiff jaw, a horse being abused in the back and mouth is a perfect example of a horse manifesting into the energetic what is happening to him on the physical plane.

3. A horse not experiencing pain in the back or mouth will quietly accept contact with the rider's hands and will be soft and round in the back and neck, as demonstrated here.

WAYS IN WHICH THE RIDER
INHERENTLY AFFECTS THE HORSE:

- Added weight – The added weight of the rider requires the horse to develop muscles and strength he would otherwise not have.
- Conflicting signals – The rider unconsciously or mistakenly pulls on a rein or grips with a leg, giving a signal she did not intend.
- Refined communication skills – The horse must learn to correctly interpret and respond to the rider's signals.
- Balance – The horse must relearn how to balance with the added weight of a rider.

WAYS IN WHICH A RIDER CAN
UNCONSCIOUSLY HARM THE HORSE:

- The rider using her hands for balance while holding the reins can accidentally jerk the horse in the mouth.
- The rider gripping with her legs in an attempt to hold on will dull the horse's sides or upset and confuse a sensitive horse.
- The rider bouncing in the saddle, thus striking the horse's back with her seat, can inflict pain and disturb the horse's balance.
- The rider asking the horse to perform beyond his mental, physical or emotional ability, can confuse, scare or injure the horse or break his spirit.
- The rider unjustly punishing the horse when he does not understand or cannot respond to her commands, can destroy his willingness to cooperate.

If she can ride in such a way as to remove the above listed obstacles, the rider will have much greater success energetically connecting with the horse. Unfortunately, with today's instruction geared toward quickly developing an attractive position for the show ring, many of the key fundamentals of an effective seat have been lost. More often than not, the absence of these basics results in upset horses and frustrated riders.

If the rider desires to achieve a seat capable of allowing her to energetically connect with the horse, she must have four basic physical factors.

PHYSICAL FACTORS REQUIRED
FOR RIDER AND HORSE ENERGETIC CONNECTION

- Unity – The rider and horse must be in unison.
- Security – The rider must be secure on the horse.
- Non-Abuse – The rider must in no way, harm, confuse, overwork or otherwise hurt or injure the horse, or treat him unfairly or unjustly.
- Effective Aids – The rider must use clear, efficient, effective aids that the horse can easily understand and to which he can easily respond.

This may sound relatively easy. Most aspiring riders have grown up watching Hollywood movies that make it appear that anyone can jump on a horse and gallop off into the sunset at a moment's notice. Others have experienced the follow-the-leader trail rides on rental horses who are so inured to interfering riders they simply ignore the conflicting signals, the jabs in their mouths and the seats pounding their backs. They just continue down the same trail with one oblivious passenger after another.

After a few of these type experiences, many sincerely believe staying on a horse is not that difficult, especially with a few lessons. Others may feel if they can control a horse and win some ribbons in the local show, they are ready to communicate on a deeper level. However many problems can be covered over or remain undiscovered during routine riding.

Free horse groundwork methods have employed an excellent environment for horses to naturally express themselves and reflect how a person affects the horse. If such a free environment is reproduced while the horse is being ridden, the horse will show the rider exactly how she is affecting him.

> **Just as on the ground, the test for riding is to remove restrictions and find out what the horse will do.**

The following exercises will assist the rider in determining how her balance, hands and legs are unconsciously affecting her horse. This will gain a true assessment of the horse's physical, mental and emotional state. *NOTE: These exercises are not recommended for beginner riders.*

Mount your horse in a medium to small size ring approximately 80 feet by 100 feet, clear of other horses and debris (this will help keep you safe). Tie a knot in the end of the reins, so you can pick them up quickly if you need to. Next drop the reins on the horse's neck, and—except for turning the horse, keeping the reins from falling over the horse's head or needing to stop the horse if he is becoming dangerously out of control—do not touch the reins. Now ride your horse at a walk, trot and canter on completely loose reins.

It is important to drop the reins on the horse's neck and let go for this experiment because often we think we are riding on completely loose reins and are not aware of what the horse actually feels. This should be done with a soft bit with no shank—such as a thick, egg butt snaffle—and without the use of a tie down or any type of martingale.

What does your horse do? Is he calm and cooperative? Does he maintain an even speed at whatever gait you put him in? A calm, responsive horse with an even, rhythmical gait usually reflects a well-balanced rider with clear signals.

Have you noticed your seat, hands and legs? Do you feel in balance and rhythm with your horse? Can you post or maintain your position in the canter with your hands on your hips? Can you ride in a two point, galloping or jumping position without using your hands to hold on?

If your horse feels out of control, rushes or runs away, this may indicate you might need some practice balancing without using your hands and legs to hold on.

It is important to realize some horses are simply more forward than others and will react that way with even the most tactful of riders. However, the above exercise will give the rider some indication of her horse's response to intended and unintended signals.

PLEASE NOTE: This exercise will only work with a healthy, sound horse. If the horse is lacking energy, is distracted or is nervous because of poor health or other issues, the rider will not gain an honest response.

> **Riding with loose reins is a good way for riders to discover how they are affecting their horses.**

*4. Riding on completely loose reins will show
the rider how she is affecting her horse.*

Riding on completely loose reins is also an excellent way to train a beginner rider in developing a functional seat without hurting the horse. By using loose reins, the rider will not risk jerking the horse in the mouth if she loses her balance. In addition, riding on loose reins allows the horse to develop straightness, independent of the rider's hands and legs. This reduces the amount of physical stress on the horse during routine riding.

Next, while still on loose reins, try turning your horse using several turns such as serpentines or squares. The turns should include several changes of direction one after another and be executed using only one rein at a time, changing hands with each turn. Leave the other rein untouched. More information on square turns can be found on page 115. This exercise is so unfamiliar for most riders it often leaves people laughing at how quickly they get their hands jumbled up.

> **Riders can easily discover if they are unconsciously depending on their hands and/or gripping legs to balance.**

These exercises will also assist a rider in determining where her horse's energy is stuck. For example, a horse who rushes, bucks or runs away may be dealing with old fears from a previous rider. He may have a sore back from an ill-fitting saddle, unbalanced feet causing his back or shoulders to be sore, or may simply not understand the rider's signals. Chapter 14 contains more detailed information on how these issues can affect the horse's ability to respond favorably to the rider.

OTHER PROBLEMS THAT A RIDER CAN DETECT BY RIDING ON LOOSE REINS

- A horse rushed through training.
- A horse with sore mouth, poll or teeth.
- A horse not physically capable of the job he is being asked to do.
- A horse who was punished when frightened or confused.
- A horse affected emotionally by a bad accident or poor riding.

A horse dealing with these physical factors will inevitably be stuck in one or more of his lower chakras. By examining the energy patterns of the chakras, the rider can easily determine where she can effectively release that blocked energy. Once the rider works with the horse to clear and open the chakras, she can achieve the connection most horsemen and women dream about and a lucky few experience *from the saddle.*

Chapter 2
Exploring the Chakras

I REMEMBER WORKING WITH A HORSE NAMED COPPER who always dragged his owner over to any blade of grass within his reach. Copper was nice and fat with a coat that shone like a new penny, but he acted as if he was starving, his head always down, trying to eat.

Copper's owner had tried everything to break his bad habit of always eating when handled, but with no success. The problem became so bad his owner felt her horse was out of control. She became afraid to handle, much less try to ride him.

I watched the horse for a while, then offered him some minerals. Poor Copper! As soon as he smelled the supplement, he shoved his head in the bucket and lapped up every granule. Then he licked the bucket clean. He was starving for minerals!

It occurred to me that with today's over processed foods, horses, like people, are getting a lot of empty calories. They are fat but are often undernourished. Chapter 14 contains more information regarding nutrition.

This malnutrition can create much havoc in the horse's first chakra, which is all about survival. Like Copper, if a horse constantly feels as if he is not getting sufficient nutrients to survive, he will focus more on eating than what the rider is trying to communicate.

In other words the horse cannot "hear" his rider past the constant pressure to find proper nutrition. This creates a tremendous block in the horse's first chakra.

The chakra energy patterns connected to the body's systems, organs and emotional and spiritual structure reflect both physical and spiritual energy. In addition to the chakras being located in basically the same areas of the human and equine bodies, the energy patterns for each chakra are similar.

Therefore the rider can also examine how she is relating to the horse by understanding her own chakra energies. Through an understanding of how these energy patterns manifest into the physical form, she can determine how to approach the horse for clearing and opening his chakras.

> **Energy patterns are similar in all beings.**

The patterns in all creatures are basically the same and appear to function the same in both humans and animals. The next page contains a chart and illustrations showing the similarities in the chakra patterns and locations of humans and horses.

Chakra	Horse	Human
1	Survival – need for food, water, shelter and safety	Family and Survival – group relations and beliefs
2	Power, procreation, place in pecking order	Money, sex, power, creativity
3	Self-confidence	Self-confidence
4	Trust, emotion, forgiveness	Trust, emotion, forgiveness
5	Will, cooperation, independence	Will, voice, self-expression, independence
6	Intellect, learning, understanding training	Intellect, wisdom
7	Relationship to the Divine, energetic connections	Relationship to the Divine, energetic connections

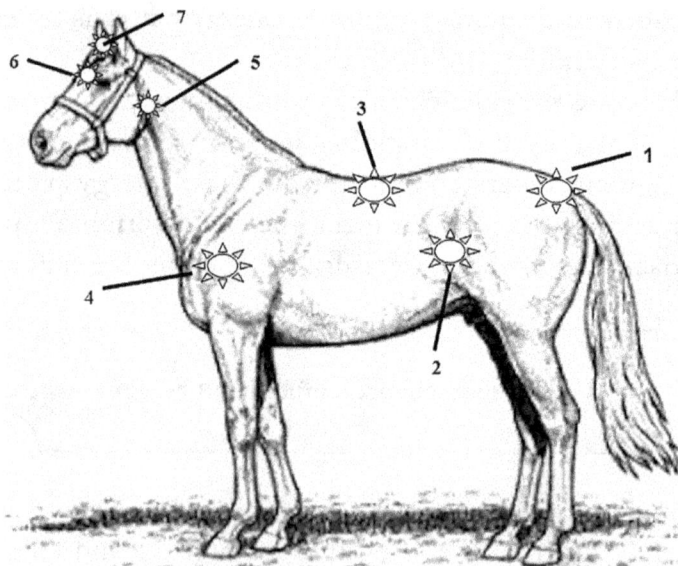

Equine Chakra Locations

1. Root
2. Sacral
3. Solar Plexus
4. Heart
5. Throat
6. Third Eye (Mind)
7. Crown

HUMAN CHAKRA
LOCATIONS

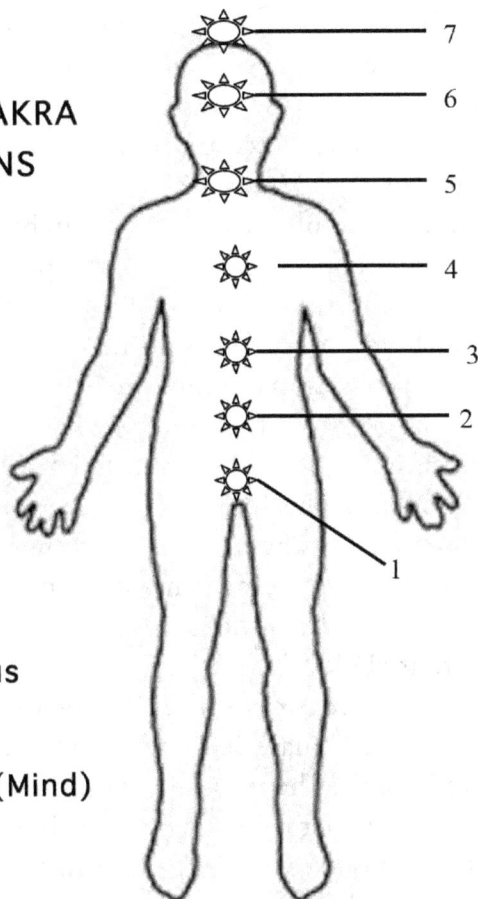

1. ROOT
2. Sacral
3. Solar Plexus
4. Heart
5. Throat
6. Third Eye (Mind)
7. Crown

Though different types of energies are identified with each chakra, the chakras are interconnected. Each chakra works in relation with the others, especially with those surrounding it. Therefore, many of the energy patterns will overlap, appear similar or connect.

In order for the rider to experience the Sacred spirit of riding, she must connect with the horse through the upper chakras, the fourth, fifth, sixth and seventh. These chakras relate horse and rider through the energetic patterns of trust, cooperation and understanding contained in these areas of the horse's body.

The lower chakras are more directly connected to the physical plane. This connection includes matters of survival and safety; the physical relationship between the horse, his environment and other horses; the physical relationship of the horse and rider; and the physical strength of the horse.

The horse must feel safe in his physical environment before he can begin to move into the upper chakras through the trust energy of the fourth chakra.

Examining how the energy patterns of the chakras manifest into physical form can help the rider recognize in which chakra the horse is operating. Once the rider can determine what energy is manifesting in the horse, she can more easily address the issues and help the horse clear and open that chakra.

The **first chakra** is the energy of survival. Does the horse have adequate food, water, shelter? Is he threatened by predators? If he is extremely jumpy at every little noise or blowing paper or is very pushy about food, it is possible the horse has some energy stuck in the first chakra.

The first chakra is the power to survive, using instinctive responses such as flight. This is where the horse lodges the information to run when he is threatened. (A horse is a prey animal whose first defense is to run away.) This energy is located in the hindquarters, which are used to propel the horse forward into a run.

The **second chakra** contains the energy of the horse's relationship within the pecking order of the herd. Place in the herd determines not only the relationship the individual horse will have with other members, but also his chances of survival and procreation (creativity). Weaker horses within a herd are forced to the outside perimeters where they are more vulnerable to predators. The stronger horses have better access to food, water and shelter.

The area of the second chakra includes the ligaments that support the sacral joint. According to equine osteopaths and noted farriers, horses with back or hindquarter problems often have a "dropped" sacrum. In other words, the muscles holding the sacral joint at the proper angle are either not sufficient or have been pulled out of place because of an accident, poor riding, riding a horse when it is too young, unbalanced shoeing or other similar causes. Many horses with a dropped sacrum appear to have issues with survival. They often have very low energy and are difficult to move forward, can be very aggressive regarding food or are very defensive around other horses. Chapter 14 discusses the dropped sacrum in more detail.

This directly ties into the energy of self-confidence found in the **third chakra.** Just as with humans, a horse who fears for his survival will often have self-confidence issues. A horse who has healthy energy patterns in its third chakra is not afraid to leave the herd when his rider asks. This type of horse is usually calm and relaxed in threatening situations.

> **NOTE:** *It is important to recognize the difference between a calm and relaxed horse and one that is in poor health. An unhealthy horse may appear calm and relaxed simply because he does not have the energy to react. Thus the well-known saying: "A lame horse is a tame horse."*

It is the area of the third chakra (just behind the saddle) that tilts upward as the horse shifts his weight and the sacral joint (the area just behind the saddle—in some horses seen as a hump or bump) is lowered. Most equestrians refer to this tilting of the sacral joint as the horse "lifting his back" when he is on the bit or collected. The horse is actually shifting his weight toward his hindquarters and lightening his forehand—which lowers his hindquarters.

It takes much self-confidence as well as physical strength for the horse to carry the weight of a rider while remaining balanced and supple, especially when on the bit or in full collection.

A horse in pain, feeling threatened, confused or otherwise unhappy with whatever the rider is doing, immediately hollows out and stiffens this part of his back. The horse is expressing a lack of strength and confidence in the actions of the rider. In the case of a horse with a dropped sacrum, this area remains hollowed out, preventing the horse from developing the muscles that allow him to easily carry weight, especially while balanced toward his hindquarters.

The **fourth chakra** is the center of trust, emotion and forgiveness. I have heard many noted horsemen and scientists say that animals or horses cannot feel emotion. However, when observing the size of the horse's heart and the size of the area of the heart chakra, I find this difficult to believe. Though their emotions may not be felt or expressed identically to human feelings, one need only be around horses to see simple reactions such as fear, anger, joy and even friendship or love.

Horses are some of the most forgiving creatures I know. Just consider how humans knowingly or unknowingly treat horses unfairly, sometimes even abusively. Through ignorance, poor riding and often, just plain poor information, we wind up confusing, hurting, scaring, starving or even unjustifiably punishing our horses.

Yet, they forgive and let us ride them again and again, even though the saddle pinches their shoulders, the bit is too severe, they can't balance because the tie down is too tight or their feet, legs, shoulders, back and hips are sore because of poorly balanced shoeing. *Horses are masters at Sacred forgiveness.*

It is through the fourth chakra that the horse begins to trust the rider. Once the horse has developed self-confidence through his third chakra, he can move into the trust energy of the fourth chakra.

It is also important to note that the fourth chakra (the energy of trust) connects the third chakra (self-confidence) with the fifth chakra (the will) in order for the horse to flex his jaw to the rider's hands.

> **The horse must develop self-confidence energy in the third chakra before he can move into the trust energy of the fourth chakra.**

The **fifth chakra** is engaged when the horse flexes to the bit, i.e., the rider's hands. This flexing is the physical manifestation of the horse accepting and willingly cooperating with the rider's commands and signals.

When a horse shies, bolts or strongly disobeys a rider, the horse throws his head up, thus raising the fifth chakra higher than the heart, and sometimes the poll which contains the seventh chakra, the connection to the Sacred. In essence the horse is raising his will above that of the rider and the Sacred.

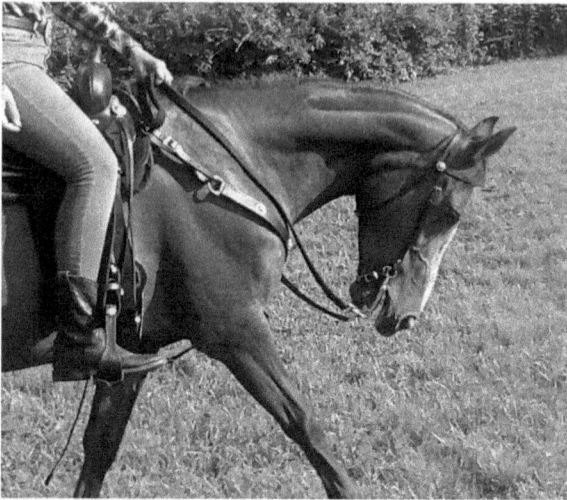

5. As shown in this photo, when a horse over-flexes and drops behind the bit, his fifth chakra is raised above the seventh, placing the horse's will above the connection with the Sacred.

The fifth chakra is also raised higher than the poll when the horse goes behind the bit, which often happens when he is over-flexed (also known as rollkur). The rider loses control when the horse goes behind the bit, and this is often a prelude to the horse "taking the bit in his teeth" and running away. The horse is actually physically removing his will from the area in which the rider can affect it.

The **sixth chakra** is the area in which the horse processes and stores the training and knowledge imparted by the rider. Once he has agreed to cooperate with the rider's signals (fifth chakra), the horse is then open to receive the knowledge to understand those commands. The horse has moved from the survival instincts of react-first-and-think-later response contained in the lower chakras to the think-first energy of the higher chakras. It is through this pausing to think process the horse learns, understands and correctly interprets the more subtle and intricate signals used when riding on contact or in semi- or full collection.

Collection is used in the higher levels of Dressage, a training system designed to develop a horse's natural abilities and teach him to understand and cooperate with the rider's requests. A high level Dressage horse, when truly collected and performing intricate maneuvers, appears to be almost in a meditative state. His eyes shine with eagerness and focus, and his ears become floppy.

That high quality of performance in the horse requires he engage the sixth chakra and think about how to respond to the rider's requests. This is similar to a state of meditation humans reach when they fully clear and engage the sixth chakra.

The **seventh chakra** is the connection with the Sacred. This capacity inspires people to enjoy horses and write songs and poetry about what it feels like to ride. We are responding to this energy when we dream of galloping through green fields, soaring over walls and executing the perfect pirouette. An Arabian proverb has said that the wind that blows through a horse's ears is the very breath of God.

Observing a horse in pure collection is the physical manifestation of seventh chakra energy. The horse is performing at a very high level. His forehand is light, and he appears to be effortlessly dancing under the rider.

The rider's hands are so soft they could be holding butterfly wings and the horse easily understands and responds to the slightest whisper of a command. Unlike when the horse travels on loose reins and his head and neck are extended, in collection, the head and neck are upright and the seventh chakra is the highest point on the horse. Therefore the seventh chakra is closer (figuratively) to the Sacred.

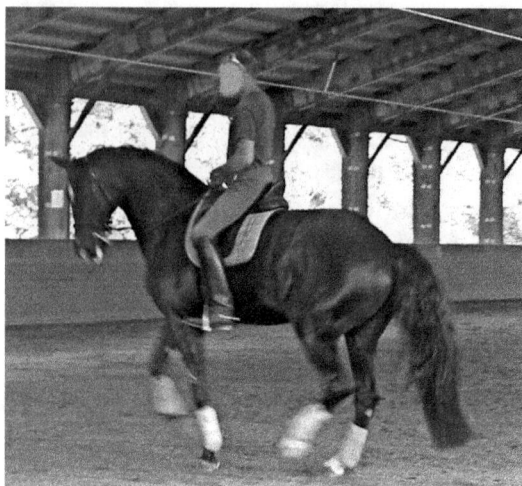

6. A horse in full collection is the physical manifestation of seventh chakra energy. As shown in this photo, his weight shifts toward the hindquarters and he appears to be lightly dancing under the rider.

Achieving true collection requires the horse be fully and healthily present in all his chakras. If the horse is in pain, is frightened, has old fears, does not understand the signals or the training or does not have the physical strength to balance a rider while collected, he will be unable to achieve true collection.

When a rider asks a horse to become collected before the horse is clear and present in all his chakras, the horse will usually resist in some way or the rider will obtain what many today are calling "false collection." False collection can be described as attempting to pull the horse onto the bit using the hands rather than riding the horse forward from the hindquarters. This false collection often results in the horse going behind the bit or over flexing as shown in figure 5.

This connection with the Sacred can also be found in semi-collection, which also engages the horse's hindquarters but to a lesser degree than full collection. High jumping can also connect the horse and rider through the Sacred as the horse goes through a moment of collection before leaving the ground. It can also be found when the horse is traveling at speed or over uneven terrain and is relaxed and fully responsive and connected to the rider.

Such connection and engagement of the chakras allows the rider to communicate softly and easily with the horse, even at speed or through dangerous or difficult terrain. The horse is quiet, calm and fully tuned and responsive to the rider's softest signals.

Even at speed and over uneven terrain the horse and rider are in perfect balance and move as if they are one. There is a rhythm and harmony between them that becomes mesmerizing.

In order to have the horse clear and entirely present in all his chakras, the horse and rider must be able to completely cooperate with one another. This allows the energy to flow fully and cleanly, not only through the horse's chakras, but between the horse and rider as well.

The horse and rider must work together as a congruent team. The horse must be able to carry the rider physically and the rider must be able to balance without interfering with the horse's natural movement and equilibrium.

Negative energy patterns stuck in the horse's chakras prevent the horse from being able to fully engage his energy and cooperate with the rider. Therefore it is important to explore solutions that help the horse clear negative patterns from his chakras and fully engage each chakra in relationship to being ridden.

7. As demonstrated by this photo, even at speed and over uneven terrain, a horse and rider who are energetically connected exhibit rhythm, harmony and balance, which is mesmerizing.

Obviously riders hold negative patterns in their chakras as well that may need to be addressed on some level to allow a healthy energy flow. There are many excellent modalities for clearing such negative patterns in humans such as yoga, acupuncture or mind-body medicine; therefore this text will not attempt to address these techniques.

However, there are some old patterns of riding that a rider may wish to explore, let go or expand with new ideas, to achieve a more perfect balance and harmony with an energetically healthy horse. Chapter 4 explores how many of these old riding patterns can affect the horse.

Chapter 3 helps the rider understand how the horse processes being ridden within the energy of each of his chakras. With this insight the rider can find a way to ride that will support the healthy clearing and opening of the horse's chakras. This understanding will also allow the rider to identify the areas in which the horse is stuck and ride in such a way as to facilitate the clearing and movement of the stuck energy.

Chapter 3
Relating the Energy Patterns

Baron was a big, beautiful, dark bay, Hanovarian gelding with a history of abuse way back in his past. He was terrified of someone touching his poll, and even though his owner had worked for years to be able to bridle him without a fight, Baron still wouldn't allow anyone to touch the top of his head for long or stand directly in front of him. He would also threaten to bite when someone touched his chest.

Though it had been many years since Baron experienced the mistreatment that caused these issues, he was still suffering from the disrupting energetic and emotional patterns of the old traumas. His owner asked me to use Axiatonal Therapy—an energy modality that clears and releases old traumas that can cause emotional distress—to try and help Baron with his old emotional and physical traumas. Chapter 15 contains more information on Axiatonal Therapy.

It took several sessions with Baron to finally get far enough into his energy patterns to address some of these issues. Then came the day I was able to reach deeply into Baron's old traumas and begin to clear away the blocks underlying many of his current troubles.

I laid one hand lightly on the white star between his eyes and the other on the side of his neck under his thick mane. I went deep, allowing the energy to circulate from my hands through his fifth chakra and back around.

The next thing I knew I was standing directly under Baron's neck with my back against his chest and my hands resting on his poll. Like an electrical current, I could feel all this incredible energy flowing and energizing both myself and Baron. The energy swirled around and between us. Baron raised his head up very high, and I allowed my hands to follow. Then he began to slowly lower his head, finally standing quietly.

Amazing! He heaved a big sigh and began taking huge deep breaths. His owner stood with her mouth open. She had never seen Baron allow anyone to touch him in that way.

This was it, the same energy I feel when I gallop a horse full blast across a field or soar over a big jump or ride a horse at full collection dancing lightly and softly between my hands and legs. It is that magical feeling one can only get in the presence of a great horse given the freedom to be magnificent.

It is this incredible flow of energy the rider feels when the horse responds to her seat, hands and legs. If the horse's chakras are clear, open and engaged, he will feel safe enough to respond from the higher chakras of trust, cooperation or thought, creating a deep energetic connection.

However if the horse has not yet learned to trust the rider or is focused on fear or pain, he will respond from a survival mode, effectively blocking a deep connection with her. If the rider understands the basic patterns connected with each chakra, she can then apply this knowledge and relate the horse's reactions to the individual chakras.

Just as with some types of ground work, allowing the horse to move freely with the rider will help clear and open the chakras. This freedom of movement allows any stuck energy to process out of the area, and the horse is able to circulate healthy energy through the chakra.

We can compare this to a wild horse who has never experienced the interfering weight and energy of the rider. Who among us has viewed pictures of wild horses galloping and not been instantly inspired by their fluidity and freedom?

This freedom is frequently seen when working with an unrestrained horse on the ground. Many have felt that clearing of energy and that open connection after spending time with a horse loose in a field or ring.

The rider who can reproduce this freedom from restraint and freedom of movement while in the saddle allows the horse to clear and open his chakras while being ridden. In order to reproduce this freedom, the rider must use a "non-interfering" seat, explained in Chapters 5 and 6, that allows the horse the maximum freedom of movement while carrying the rider.

> If the rider can interpret the signs of an energetically healthy horse, she is better equipped to identify underlying issues preventing him from moving forward in his training.

Once the horse has begun to clear and open his chakras, the rider can move to a trusting, a cooperative and, ultimately, an enlightened seat. Chapter 10 contains more information on how the non-interfering seat is used in the phases of communication.

If the rider can interpret the physical signs of an energetically healthy horse under saddle, she can identify underlying issues preventing the horse from moving forward in his training. The rider can then heal these blocks and establish trust and cooperation in the horse rather than relying on force to subdue him. The physical characteristics of an energetically healthy horse are the following:

First Chakra – The first chakra contains the energy of survival through the horse's ability to access resources and the traits of his breed. It is the horse's physical ability to process food, find water and shelter and avoid predators that helps him stay alive. For example, Thoroughbreds may be able to outrun a fast predator, but they are not as hardy and need more food than a wild Mustang, which can survive on sparse prairie grass.

In physical form this chakra generates the amount of speed, agility or strength the horse needs to either flee or fight a predator. Located in the hindquarters, the horse's source of power, it is in the first chakra where the horse initially ignites or converts energy into physical movement.

The horse can begin his movement either through a state of fear or through a more desirable and healthy state of relaxed confidence. First chakra healthy energy manifests into the physical as calm, relaxed, efficient movement in the horse.

The rider can begin teaching the horse this calm, relaxed, free movement on the lunge line and then reproduce such movement from the saddle by using a non-interfering seat. Once the horse creates the healthy energy in the hindquarters, the rider can engage that energy through the second chakra and ask the horse to move the energy forward.

Second Chakra – The second chakra is the area from which the horse relates to other individuals. If the first chakra is the horse's engine, the second chakra is the drive shaft. It is in the second chakra where the horse decides in which direction the energy will flow. Will he go up, sideways, backward or forward?

Once the horse converts the energy in the hindquarters, it is through the second chakra the energy is engaged. The physical manifestation of this engagement is the horse using his hocks to thrust forward and his stifles to pull the leg under the body. This movement of the hind leg under the body is called engagement and creates the forward movement.

As with the first chakra, this engagement of second chakra energy can be through fear or can be relaxed and confident. The rider can again use the non-interfering seat to allow the horse movement free of pain or restraint. This manifests in the physical as a relaxed, calm, efficient movement from the horse.

It is important to remember the second chakra is about personal, one-on-one relationships. It is here where the horse decides if the rider is a threat or friend. The rider's relationship with the horse on the ground can be strongly enhanced by first developing healthy boundaries, described in Chapter 13.

It is also through the second chakra the horse relates directly to the rider everything that happens to him such as fear, pain confusion or other threats to his safety.

For example, the horse doesn't understand his back hurts because the saddle doesn't fit. He only knows that it hurts when someone rides him.

Once the horse feels safe with the rider, he will calmly and willingly engage his energy and move it forward through the second chakra. As the horse moves the energy forward, it is time to develop the horse's physical ability to balance the rider and carry himself with quality of movement. This engages the horse's third chakra.

Third Chakra – The third chakra is the energy of self-confidence. It is here the horse determines if, and how, he will respond to a potential threat. If the horse experiences fear, pain, confusion or other threats to his safety, he will revert to the survival "flight, fight or freeze" mode and manifest this physically by running away, becoming "desensitized" or fighting the rider by rearing, bucking, kicking, biting, pushing or other forms of defense.

For example, when a horse is ready to fight by bucking, he lifts his lumbosacral joint, the area just behind the saddle. Horsemen call this a "cold backed" horse.

It is in this area of the back the horse transforms the power and forward movement from the hindquarters through to the forehand and either engages the shoulders to move forward or rounds the back in preparation of rearing, bucking, backing up or jumping sideways.

This area underneath and just behind the saddle also contains the muscles and ligaments that help support the rider. If the horse feels safe with and accepts the rider, he relaxes this area of his back and allows the energy to flow freely through to the shoulders and completes his steps forward. In a relaxed, healthy, happy horse, this area of the back develops a quality of muscle, giving what many horsemen term a "good top line."

It is through the third chakra the horse manifests the ability to perform the *higher quality* of movement desired in good riding. By engaging healthy third chakra energy, the horse develops the physical strength, agility and balance necessary for a higher quality performance.

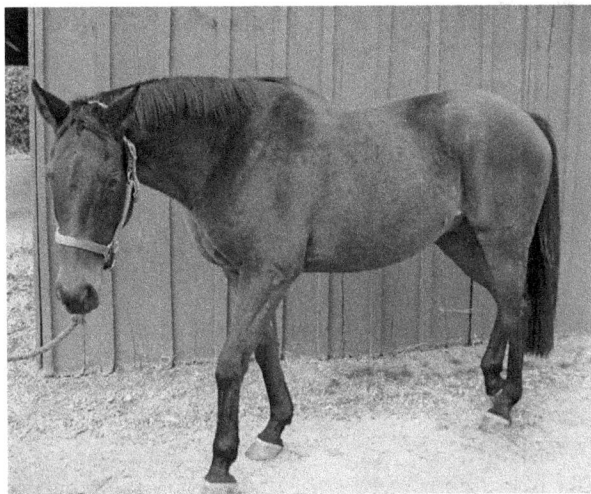

*8. As shown here, a horse with a good top line has well
-developed, quality core muscles he uses to carry the rider.*

A horse with a poor self-confidence will not be able to
develop these physical qualities because he will be weak in his
back. This weakness manifests in a hollowed out, stiff back,
which prevents the horse from building the quality of muscle
to perform at higher levels.

To clear and open the horse's third chakra, the rider must
first protect that area of the horse's back from pain or abuse.
Examples of such abuse are a rider hitting the horse in the
back with her seat or using an ill-fitting saddle. Another
important factor is to allow the horse to lift and stretch
the muscles from his shoulders through the thoracic area
(the barrel) and activate his core abdominal muscles. This
removes the pressure on the horse's back and allows the
horse's core to support the rider. The easiest way to protect
the horse's back and allow room for this stretching is for
the rider to use a non-interfering seat, which allows the

rider to remove her weight from this area of the horse's back so he can engage his core muscles.

The horse will initiate this stretching by extending his head and neck out and down. Riding the horse on loose reins, or a long rein as used in early Dressage schooling, allows this stretching to begin in the jaw and neck and continue through to the thoracic area.

As the horse gains confidence in his ability to balance and carry the rider through the development of quality muscles in his core, he will begin to lift his head and gain more confidence, thus increasing the engagement of the third chakra energies.

As with humans, the horse must first gain self-confidence before he can truly trust another. With strong self-confidence the horse can trust the rider to make decisions. It is this trust that engages the energy of the fourth chakra.

9. A non-interfering seat, as demonstrated in this photo, allows the rider to remove her weight and root chakra from the horse's third chakra.

Fourth Chakra – The fourth chakra is the area where the horse decides to trust the rider. It is through this chakra the horse connects the self-confidence of the third chakra to the fifth chakra allowing for cooperation with the rider. The horse must trust the rider before he will cooperate with her.

In order to manifest the trust energy into the physical plane, the rider must prevent the horse from experiencing pain, confusion or betrayal at her hands. She must be able to ride without bouncing in the saddle, using the reins to balance or holding on with her legs.

Her signals must be clear and she must never ask the horse to perform any task for which he is not physically, mentally or emotionally capable or prepared. A green broke, three-year-old horse does not have the mental, emotional or physical capacity to jump four feet or perform a collected canter. This would cause the horse emotional stress, fear, sore muscles and confusion and violate his ability to trust.

A horse constantly experiencing such pain, confusion, unjustified punishment or being asked to perform beyond his ability will either tune the rider out and ignore her commands or simply try to run away.

By using a functional seat and effective aids, the rider not only prevents unintentional abuse or confusion but refrains from interfering with the horse's natural movement, allowing the chakras to clear and open. A functional, non-interfering seat such as the forward balance position exercise described in Chapter 6, makes the horse feel safe and creates an environment in which the horse can trust the rider.

A non-interfering seat will also clear the rider's root chakra from the horse's heart chakra and allow the energy to flow from the horse's first chakra through to his fourth. In the forward balance position, the rider is also placing her heart chakra closer to the horse's heart chakra.

It is often when working in fourth chakra energy that the rider's inability to trust becomes apparent. This usually shows up in the clutching or gripping leg of a rider who does not feel secure in the saddle.

A rider who grips or holds on with the leg out of insecurity or fear is clutching the horse's heart chakra and creates an energy block for both the horse and rider. Some horses will respond to this gripping by not moving freely forward, others will interpret it as a go signal and increase their speed or run away.

If the rider can acquire a relaxed, secure, non-abusive position, the horse will respond by engaging the heart chakra energy. The rider now changes from a non-interfering seat to a cooperative seat and rides sitting in the saddle while on the flat. The horse is also ready for the rider to take a soft contact of the reins and begin to connect the horse's lower chakras with the horse's higher chakras through the fourth chakra energy.

This opens the door to the incredible trust and partnership for which so many riders are searching. It is through this partnership the horse begins to cooperate with the rider's wishes. This cooperation is the physical manifestation of fifth chakra energy.

Fifth Chakra – The fifth chakra is engaged when the horse relaxes, flexes his jaw and cooperates with the rider's signals. This flexing of the jaw requires an engagement of the horse's back—often referred to as "through the back." This engagement is the energy (often called impulsion) flowing forward from the horse's hindquarters. The energy engages and connects the third and fifth chakras and allows the horse to carry the rider and himself in a more balanced manner.

This is the beginning of work "on the bit" that leads to semi- and full collection. When a horse truly relaxes his jaw and comes through the back, the feel of the reins is so light and soft as to feel effortless. The rider receives the total and instantaneous cooperation of the horse.

Riding on loose reins is ideal for the clearing and opening of the fifth chakra. For less experienced riders, this creates the same results used by advanced Dressage riders who develop "looseness" in the horse with a semi-loose rein (often called a long rein) or a soft, light and flowing contact. These advanced riders understand the absolute necessity of having the horse loose and relaxed in order to build the proper muscles to carry the rider while on the bit or collected.

The clearing and opening of the fifth chakra physically manifests in the horse's ability to stretch his head and neck forward and down, allowing stretching and development of quality core muscles. Then, as the horse builds the muscles used to balance with a rider (third chakra) the horse returns his head and neck to a more normal position with the head above the line of the withers.

10. As shown here, a horse with an open fifth chakra is relaxed in his jaw and has a soft, cooperative mouth.

The engagement of the fifth chakra connects the fifth and third chakras through the fourth (the heart), and the horse uses his physical strength and agility to softly and precisely cooperate with the rider's signals.

The rider no longer uses voice except occasionally in schooling. As the horse softly responds to her signals, she switches from using her hands to primitively steer the horse, to using her hands to contain or release energy. The rider uses her legs to create energy in the horse's hindquarters, then contains or releases it to affect the horse's responses. It is through this containment and release of the energy that the rider is able to softly and more precisely create higher quality responses in the horse.

This soft, precise quality of cooperation and communication is the sixth chakra energy of mind and thought.

Sixth Chakra – The sixth chakra is the center of understanding the rider's signals. Once the horse is able to physically respond to the rider's signals and is willing to join his will in cooperation with the rider, the horse must now process the rider's requests through his mind rather than use more primitive flight, fight or freeze responses.

The physical manifestation of engaging the sixth chakra is noticed when the horse switches from the instinctive "react first" response of the lower chakras to a "think first" response of the higher chakras. This is reflected in the rider's use of a cooperative seat with hands and legs collaborating with each other and the horse's movements.

The horse now has the physical and mental ability to understand and translate the rider's softer, more subtle signals into a higher quality of movement and response. As the horse's understanding and physical ability increase, the communication becomes even more subtle. This moves the horse into his seventh chakra.

Seventh Chakra – The seventh chakra is the direct connection to the Sacred. Once all the horse's chakras are open, the energy has a clear channel in which it can flow from the hindquarters, first chakra, through to the forehand, seventh chakra, and back in full circle.

This free flow of energy allows the horse to reach a high level of performance such as semi- and full collection, high jumping or more advanced communication at speed. The physical manifestation of seventh chakra energy is a horse who is light, soft and responsive to the rider's every wish. The horse is calm, alert, agile and cooperative.

A rider engages the horse's seventh chakra in the physical form by requesting energy from the hindquarters and allowing that energy to flow freely up the horse's chakras and through her hands. The rider then either directs the energy into a high level of performance, as in collection, or allows the energy to express itself through speed or jumping.

> **NOTE:** *It is important to realize that this level of speed is not the same as that of a frightened horse running away. When using seventh chakra energy through speed, the horse is listening and cooperating with the rider. A frightened horse running away is steeped in first and second chakra energy and is not listening to the rider.*

Riding in the seventh chakra is more about engaging and working with the horse's energy than signaling the horse. High-level Dressage rides are about allowing a high quality and a high *quantity* of forward energy to flow through the horse and rider, connecting them as one. Riders who have felt an energetic connection with the horse's seventh chakra often comment that the horse seems to read their minds because the horse responds so quickly and easily to the slightest signal.

> **Riders engaging the horse's seventh chakra often feel the horse can read their minds.**

The Sacred Connections Horsemanship system of riding and training is the easiest, fastest and most effective way for most riders to accomplish the clearing and opening of the horse's chakras. It combines the chakra energy work with elements of Forward Riding, which is based on forward balance, forward schooling and forward control. Both begin with a non-interfering seat—up off the saddle.

It is important to note that many advanced, talented Dressage riders have developed the ability to ride using a non-interfering seat while sitting in the saddle. These riders have spent years perfecting an effective seat that does not abuse the horse's back and allows the horse the freedom to develop his back muscles. However, I do not recommend most riders attempt to open the horse's chakras using this seated approach for starting a green horse.

The classical system of Dressage training was originally designed to be studied by a military rider who rode eight hours a day, five to six days a week, *for several years*. Most of today's riders simply cannot invest the time or patience every day for years to gain the experience required to use a Dressage seat for opening the horse's chakras.

Therefore today's riders need a proven system that is fast, easy and effective. By using Sacred Connections Horsemanship, riders can easily develop an effective seat and method of communication. This communication will allow them to quickly clear and open the horse's heart chakra, thus allowing them to experience moments of Sacred connection with their horse without having to be highly advanced. The foundation for the effective seat and communication used in Sacred Connections Horsemanship is developed through the Four Key Essentials described in the following chapter. Chapters 5 and 6 will illustrate how to create these essentials using simple exercises. Following this system, riders can quickly advance through the non-interfering, trusting, cooperative and enlightened phases while they work with the energy in their horse's corresponding chakras. The rider can use this foundation for any style of riding and still find that Sacred connection with her horse.

Part II

Mapping Trails

Chapter 4
Building Trust through
Four Key Essentials

ACCORDING TO THE AFFILIATED NATIONAL RIDING Commission, Olympic rider Lendon Gray once commented, "Prove to me that you can ride on loose reins." Gray went on to state that many riders today have lost the ability to ride "non-interferingly."

Gray was commenting on the fact that most riders interfere so greatly with their horses that the horses cannot move efficiently, much less naturally. Yet this is where a truly functional seat must begin. In order for a horse to perform well, he must first be able to move as naturally as possible while carrying a rider.

Freedom of natural movement is popular in many "at liberty" techniques used in groundwork today. (The horse is allowed to be loose in a ring or pen with no lead rope or lunge line while the handler asks him for different movements.)

Sacred Connections Horsemanship adds this element of liberty for the horse while being ridden. Riding on loose reins with a completely non-interfering seat allows the mounted horse the same type of liberty as the above-mentioned groundwork techniques. As Gray was suggesting, riding on a completely loose rein and with a non-interfering seat, gives the horse the liberty to express himself and be honest about how the rider is affecting him.

Regardless of the style of riding or type of saddle, if a rider can ride in unison with her horse, be secure in the saddle, ride in a way as not to hurt the horse and be able to clearly communicate with the horse, she will achieve a more natural response.

Employing the four keys of unity, security, non-abuse and effective communication helps the rider develop a non-interfering seat and the ability to allow her horse to be completely honest. Through this freedom to be honest, the horse learns to trust the rider. As stated in Chapter 1, riding correctly is the physical manifestation of trust between the two.

When a rider and horse trust each other and can communicate through that trust, they appear to be working together as a team or as one. The horse softly, quickly and quietly responds to the rider's commands. The rider is in balance with the horse and flows with his movements. The entire picture appears smooth and effortless.

This may sound simple at first, but if the rider takes the time to observe numerous horses' performances with an educated eye, she will see it is not often accomplished. Unfortunately, many riders attempt to achieve the above by mimicking what correct riders *look* like without understanding how the rider's position is actually functioning.

These attempts to adopt an *image* of riding rather than a functional position usually result in a stiff rider who is often out of balance or rhythm with the horse. Such riders can rarely use their hands or legs independently from their bodies, resulting in conflicting signals to the horse.

IN ORDER TO ACHIEVE A NATURAL RESPONSE FROM THE HORSE, THE RIDER MUST BE ABLE TO:

- Balance on a moving horse without using her hands or gripping with her legs to stay on.
- Ride in such a way that she does not interfere with the horse's natural movement.
- Communicate in such a way that does not confuse or hurt the horse.
- Clear any of her old energy patterns that do not support the first three achievements.

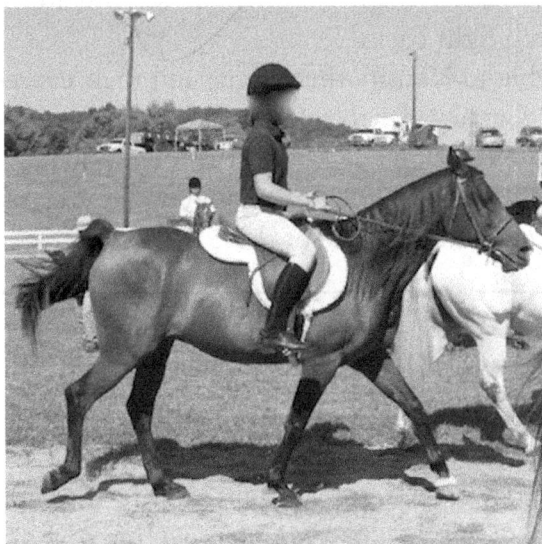

11. As shown here, attempts to adopt a correct riding image rather than a functional position usually result in a stiff rider who is often out of balance or rhythm with the horse.

When confused or hurt by an interfering rider, the horse will focus on his own welfare and remain stuck in his lower chakras. The rider's effect on the horse will typically manifest in the horse's stiffness, resistance and uncooperative responses. In extreme cases the horse will display dangerous behavior such as bolting, rearing or bucking.

Identifying the Weakness and Gaps that Develop from Riding for Looks Rather than Function

Horses always tell us when they are confused, frightened or uncomfortable—but one must be able to read the signs. Quiet, tolerant horses tend to ignore the rider's conflicting signals and are often accused of having a hard mouth or dull sides or of being "stubborn." More sensitive horses will attempt to run away or even fight back.

Being able to identify these signs and their causes requires the ability for the rider to see beyond conveying a fashionable image of the rider on the horse, "the look" popular in today's show ring. Identifying and understanding these signs gives the rider a way to address some of these issues.

> Horses always tell us when they are confused, frightened or uncomfortable.

Signs a horse is confused:
A confused horse will not respond as the rider wishes because he simply cannot understand the signals. A very quiet and tolerant horse may ignore the rider and go where he pleases, or a less tolerant horse may grab the bit in his teeth and run away. This latter behavior is the result of feeling threatened by something he does not understand.

Running away can take many forms beyond just galloping very fast. A horse can run away by simply increasing speed within a gait or traveling in an unrhythmic gait. If the horse cannot go forward, he may back up, rear, buck, jump, pop a shoulder in a turn or scoot sideways.

Signs a horse is scared:

A scared horse will usually attempt to run away. The very first action of a scared horse is to throw his head up and push all his weight to his hindquarters (first and second chakra survival energy). By shifting his weight toward the hindquarters, the horse can then launch himself into a run. Other signs of a frightened horse will be very similar to those of confusion such as rearing, bucking or backing up.

Another reaction of a scared horse is to go into the numb or "freeze" mode of "flight," "fight" or "freeze." These three instinctive responses to what is believed to be a mortal threat are common in all prey animals. Freezing usually happens when the horse can no longer run away or fight and simply surrenders to his fate.

When in freeze mode, the horse is basically shut down or "numb" to most things around him. He appears quiet and docile and will tolerate strange things, such as plastic bags, blankets waving or a saddle and rider.

This method of placing a horse in freeze mode is commonly used in many natural horsemanship techniques in which the horse is "worked"—run around a round pen or back and forth on the end of a long rope—until he can no longer run. For more discussion on natural horsemanship, see page 53.

This freeze mode is also sometimes induced in the practice of "desensitizing" a horse. The horse is placed in a small enclosure such as a round pen or restrained so he cannot run away. He is then "sacked out" or exposed to a flapping blanket, plastic bags, tarps, large balls, an opening and closing umbrella or other strange objects until he becomes numb to such objects.

This desensitizing a horse by repeatedly working him until he surrenders or submits has gained a lot of recent popularity, but can, unfortunately, be easily misused. The horse can be overworked and soured.

A desensitized horse, or a horse in freeze mode, is not the same as a trained horse. Often when worked with the desensitizing method, the horse will come out of freeze mode and will go into flight or fight mode, either running away or even threatening the handler. Though this desensitizing technique creates an extremely submissive horse, the horse is still in a state of fear and therefore cannot move into his higher chakras, which is required in order to create a bond of trust between horse and rider.

Natural horsemanship showed us an alternative to breaking, busting or bucking out a horse. However, if the rider desires a deeper connection with her mount, the method—like so many—leaves much room for improvement. By keeping the horse in the survival instinct of the first chakra (flight, fight, freeze) this method prevents the higher chakra connections of trust, thinking and Sacred energy. Though it is an improvement on the physical aspect of earlier breaking methods, natural horsemanship can affect the horse mentally and emotionally, preventing him from moving into the trust and thought energy of his higher chakras.

NOTE: *Many natural horsemanship techniques use the freeze mode to force the horse into a state of submissiveness in which he appears to be quite docile. In such techniques the horse is "worked"—run around and around a round pen, or back and forth on the end of a long rope—until he tires out and submits or somehow manages to discover what the human is wanting. From the horse's perspective, he is trapped in an enclosed area, or captured by the rope, with a carnivore (human) chasing him.*

The horse runs until he cannot run any more, then turns "at bay" to face the handler. This is fight mode. When the carnivore does not engage the horse in battle, the horse then shifts into freeze mode and submits himself to the predator (human). When moving into this submissive state, the horse appears to be very docile and easy to handle, and will often walk up to the carnivore.

To novices, this can look as if the horse is "joining" or bonding with the human. Yet a closer examination reveals the horse is not present in his mind and spirit and is actually submitting himself to whatever fate awaits him, even if that is death. In other words the horse is in "freeze" mode and is numb to any further harm that may come to him.

While this technique appears to be much kinder than breaking a horse to saddle by bucking him out, it lacks certain elements of quality horsemanship and classical training that are so important to the healthy development of the horse's chakra energies. Unfortunately, many natural horsemanship techniques use these types of quick fixes, along with gimmicks and/or gadgets—such as sticks or weighted reins—rather than going through a logical, systematic progression of training that addresses the horse's mental, physical, emotional and energetic needs.

Signs a horse is uncomfortable or in pain:

A horse who does not want to move freely forward may be unwilling because it hurts to move. The old saying, "A lame horse is a tame horse," is very true, especially for many cold-blooded horses.

A sensitive horse who snaps or bites when being saddled or ridden, bucks, tosses his head or swishes his tail, may have a saddle pinching his back or shoulders. A horse who will not stand still for mounting is often in pain from an ill-fitting saddle or sore back.

A horse who bucks or runs away may be suffering from a rider's seat hitting his back or a rider's legs squeezing his sides. Other horses may react to a rider's legs constantly gripping or squeezing their sides by slowing down or not moving forward.

A horse who throws his head up and hollows out his back may be showing signs of pain caused by a rider hitting the horse in the back or jerking the horse in the mouth. A too severe bit or teeth that need care can also cause this reaction.

These are some basic signs of pain, fear or confusion we often miss in our daily riding. If the horse is not "head-bobbing lame," many horsemen and equine practitioners do not see the pain. Other basic signs may be tail swishing, pawing, not standing still or head tossing. Chapter 14 offers more information on unsoundness and pain.

Armed with this information and new insight, the rider can visit a local horse show to see horses with their heads in the air, backs stiff and tails swishing. She may observe many horses wearing martingales (tie downs); horses wearing severe bits; horses popping their shoulders in turns; riders hitting the horses' backs with their seats; and riders with a death grip on the reins, trying to slow down their horses.

12. A horse who throws his head up and hollows out his back may be showing signs of pain caused by a rider hitting the horse in the back or jerking the horse in the mouth.

Undoubtedly these riders are doing their best using what they have been taught. So many instructors today are teaching riders to look "correct" for the show ring, they have forgotten the "functionality" of riding.

In addition, many riders are feeling so much pressure to win, they are forgetting the reason they wanted to ride in the first place. They have lost touch with the fact their horses are not enjoying being hit in the back, jerked in the mouth or confused by conflicting signals.

> **Many riders are feeling pressure to win in the shows, forgetting the reason they wanted to ride in the first place.**

Feeling safe while looking good:

Another challenge for riders today is the problem of feeling insecure in the saddle. By focusing on how the rider should "look" in the saddle, many instructors have forgotten the importance of—or even how to teach—a *secure, functional* seat.

Many riders are able to connect very well with their horses through ground work. Yet when it comes time to ride, tension coils in their gut, their legs grip the horse, and they find themselves clinging to the saddle—afraid to leave the ring or, in some cases, even mount their horse.

They become increasingly frustrated as the instructor tells them to "keep your ear, shoulder, hip and heel in a straight line," "keep your heels down," "sit tall and allow your hips and pelvis to accompany the movements of the horse's back," "keep a straight line from the horse's mouth through your hands and elbows and follow the movements of the horse's head with your hands," and various other versions of trying to get a beginner or a frightened rider to learn to balance and control a moving horse all at once.

Is it any wonder more riders do not achieve the energetic purity we all dream of when we first think of riding? Is it any wonder many riders are frustrated because they cannot transfer the wonderful relationship they have on the ground to the saddle? Are we doomed to never have that taste of divinity that can only be grasped from the back of a horse?

> **Riders need a clear, proven system that develops balance, stability and security in the saddle.**

In order for the rider to have a deep connection and sacred experience with her horse, she needs to feel safe and secure in the saddle. If the rider is distracted with concerns about staying on the horse, she will be closed to an energetic connection.

All functional seats, regardless of the saddle used, contain the Four Key Essentials.

Safety and security in the saddle begin with developing a *functional seat that does not hurt the horse.* In addition to looking good, a truly effective seat has Four Key Essentials that guarantee the rider stability in the saddle, easy communication with the horse and the connection and clarity needed to achieve a higher energetic relationship while riding.

THESE FOUR KEY ESSENTIALS ARE:

1. Unity of the horse and rider in motion
2. Security of the rider in the saddle
3. Non-abuse of the horse by the rider's seat, hands or legs
4. Efficient and effective use of aids (signals) for communication

A truly effective seat applies to any style of riding. A rider whose seat functions well can swiftly and effortlessly change from any riding style to any other style because all effective positions, regardless of the saddle used, contain these Four Key Essentials.

For example, an effective rider who uses the forward seat can easily adapt to Western or Dressage because the rider develops a long, deep leg that allows her to stay secure in the saddle and in balance with the horse, rather than just following a fad for the show ring. This long, deep leg is applicable to any style of riding, regardless of stirrup length or saddle. An effective rider can easily and swiftly change her dynamic ability from balancing up out of the saddle when riding faster gaits or over uneven terrain and jumps to sitting deep in the saddle and shifting the horse's balance more toward the hindquarters.

A truly functional seat is an absolute necessity for connecting with the horse energetically. If the rider causes the horse to lose balance, become confused or feel pain, the horse will be distracted by the physical problems he is experiencing and will be unable to connect with the rider energetically. If the rider is afraid of falling off or cannot get the horse to follow her commands, she will also be stuck in the physical.

13. Forward Seat
The photograph demonstrates the forward pelvic tilt in the rider and the alignment of the rider's heel, hip and shoulder. The rider's balance is slightly forward.

14. Dressage Seat
The photograph demonstrates the same forward pelvic tilt and heel–hip–shoulder alignment, but the rider's balance is more centered, and the stirrup is slightly longer.

15. Western Seat
The Western seat is a duplication of the Dressage seat, regardless of saddle style. The forward pelvic tilt and the heel–hip–shoulder alignment are identical. The balance is centered.

Both the horse and the rider, concerned with physical survival issues such as pain, confusion or staying in the saddle, will relate to each other purely from the first and second chakras, often in the negative. For example, the horse simply cannot understand the difference between a pull on the reins to request a turn and a pull on the reins to help the rider maintain her balance. From the horse's point of view, both pulls feel the same.

> **From the horse's point of view, there is no difference between a pull on the reins to turn the horse and a pull on the reins to help the rider maintain her balance.**

By understanding and employing the Four Key Essentials, a rider can begin to elevate her ride past the physical into the energetic.

Defining the Four Key Essentials:

1. UNITY OF THE HORSE AND RIDER IN MOTION – ENCOMPASSES ALL CHAKRAS, BUT PRIMARILY FOURTH AND SEVENTH CHAKRA ENERGY

The expression of being "one with the horse" is a Western world expression of riding in the seventh chakra. Many riders describe this as an esoteric ideal they dream of achieving "some day." However, few riders, or even trainers, can actually define what it means.

Although being one with the horse is primarily fourth and seventh chakra energy, like all energy, it also manifests in the physical. The physical manifestation of unity can be interpreted as the rider moving her body in balance, rhythm and harmony with the horse's movement.

For example, if the horse is moving at speed, his weight will be more on the forehand. Therefore the rider's upper body is inclined forward enough to keep her weight centered or balanced over the horse's center of gravity. If the horse is performing Dressage maneuvers and his weight is more toward his hindquarters, the rider will sit deep in the saddle with her torso more upright and her balance more centered.

When the rider is in rhythm with the horse, she is relaxed enough for her ankles, knees, hips, waist, arms and hands to move in sync with the horse's movements. This balance and movement creates a shared rhythm, fluidity and synchronicity while the horse is in motion.

A rider who is not in rhythm with her horse will disturb the horse's movement, causing him to speed up, slow down or even break his gait. Such disturbances are a direct result of a non-functional position of the rider.

When a horse and rider have unity together in motion, they will have balance and rhythm and appear relaxed and harmonious in their movement. The movement of both horse and rider appears fluid, in sync and effortless.

The balance, rhythm and synchronicity all work together to create a harmonious flow of energy between the horse and rider. This harmonious flow of energy is the physical manifestation of unity of the horse and rider in motion.

> **When a horse and rider have unity in motion, their movements will appear fluid, in sync and effortless.**

2. SECURITY OF THE RIDER IN THE SADDLE – FIRST, SECOND AND THIRD CHAKRA ENERGY

Security directly relates to first, second and third chakra energy. A secure rider can adapt to, and not interfere with, the horse's natural movement (first and second chakras). A secure rider also does not unintentionally bounce on the horse's back with her seat (third chakra). This protects the third chakra and allows it to open and develop the horse's self-confidence.

A rider who is truly secure in the saddle can stay with the horse at all speeds regardless of terrain. The truly secure rider uses weight and balance to stay on and therefore can move freely with the horse over uneven terrain, at speed and over jumps. Such a rider can usually stay on a horse when the horse rears, bucks, shies, bolts or otherwise exhibits less than perfect behavior.

The truly secure rider uses little muscular grip to stay on because muscular grip will tire her out during long rides and causes both the rider and horse to be stiff or tense. In addition, the truly secure rider does not need her hands or legs to hold on and thus does not interfere with the balancing gestures of the horse's head and neck or with the horse's clear understanding of signals. Chapter 5 describes how a secure rider uses balance, weight, relaxation and spring to stay in the saddle rather than trying to grip with her legs or balance with her hands.

A secure rider will feel bold and confident in her riding (third chakra) and will create a bold, confident horse. I find it very interesting that a non-secure rider will inevitably bounce on the horse's back, hitting him in the area of the third chakra, thus affecting the horse's confidence.

3. NON-ABUSE OF THE HORSE BY THE RIDER'S SEAT, HANDS OR LEGS – FOURTH AND FIFTH CHAKRA ENERGY

Non-abuse of the horse is primarily a fourth chakra energy because it is about building trust. It also includes the fifth chakra in that the horse will only cooperate with a rider he can trust.

A rider who is non-abusive to her horse is careful to ride without using her hands or legs for balance and is secure enough in the saddle that her seat does not strike the horse in the back. Such a rider's arms and legs work independently from her body, preventing her from unintentionally interfering with or harming her horse.

In addition, the rider is aware of her horse's level of training and physical condition. She does not ask the horse to perform beyond his physical, mental and emotional capability, thus preserving his trust that she will keep him safe.

Chapter 13 provides a full definition of abuse as used in this text.

4. THE RIDER'S AIDS ARE PLACED IN A POSITION TO BE USED EFFECTIVELY – SIXTH CHAKRA ENERGY

In order to be functional, a rider must be able to communicate with her horse in a *way the horse can understand*. This is a sixth chakra energy involving communication and training. By learning natural aids that make sense to the horse and result in a natural response from the horse, the rider can communicate her commands easily and clearly.

Once the horse has opened his fifth chakra to the rider (willingly cooperating with the rider), it is her responsibility to use an understandable system of communication. By doing so, the rider allows the horse the room to enter the state of clarity necessary to achieve seventh chakra energy.

Using the aids efficiently and effectively means they are soft and subtle. Such aids, described in Chapter 11, make it appear as if the horse and rider are communicating almost telepathically.

While each of the Four Key Essentials connects primarily with specific chakras, they are all necessary for development of *all* the horse's chakras. The rider simply uses each essential in a manner that corresponds to the horse's level of training. For example, in using Essential #4 (effective aids), a squeezing leg is more effective for a horse in later stages of training, while a tapping or kicking leg is the most effective for a green horse.

Chapter 11 contains more information regarding leg aids and their application.

In order to achieve the Four Key Essentials, a rider uses Seven Basic Elements, discussed in the next chapter, to create a functional position. Applying these seven elements allows the rider to build a strong, effective position that contains all the desirable elements for her to become one with the horse's natural movement. This encourages the horse to open his chakras and connect with the rider on much deeper levels.

Chapter 5
Basic Elements for Chakra Riding

"THAT WAS SO MUCH MORE FUN THAN GOING AROUND in circles with someone yelling at you to keep your heels down," said Hailey with a big smile. She had just finished a lesson trotting and cantering up and down hills.

Hailey was expressing relief from the frustration so many riders encounter with modern methods of riding instruction. Such riders receive a lot of practice in making their position "look" good, but are not able to experience the joy of feeling safe in the saddle outside a ring. Indeed, even many trail riders today will not trot, canter or gallop down hills.

The frustration these riders feel is the lack of a methodical system that clearly explains and helps them ride a functional position that is secure and effective. Hailey used the lesson on the hills to develop balance in motion, a secure base of support in her heels (correct weight distribution), spring and rhythm, allowing her to move freely as one with her horse.

Many riders dream of this freedom of movement and unity of motion, but few actually achieve it.

Through the development of Seven Basic Elements of a functional position, a rider can gain a secure and effective seat that allows her to have the fun Hailey experienced in her ride. The balance in motion, correct weight distribution, spring and rhythm that Hailey used are some of the Seven Basic Elements that make up the Four Key Essentials of a functional position discussed in the previous chapter.

Certain details of these elements may vary slightly depending on the type or style of riding. For example, a saddle seat rider who rides smooth-gaited horses in the ring, a Dressage rider who rides in a flat arena and a Western rider working cattle all use a deep seat and a long stirrup length. Whereas a forward seat rider riding cross country or a jockey riding at speed require a shorter stirrup length in order to be able to stand up and balance at speed and/or over uneven terrain.

The similar element here is that whether riding Dressage or racing the Kentucky Derby, the rider will still move in rhythm and balance with the horse, be relaxed, maintain spring in her joints, place her aids in position to be used effectively and distribute her weight evenly.

Though the riders of these various styles may have a shorter or longer stirrup, always sit in the saddle or occasionally stand up in their stirrups, each rider must use the Four Key Essentials and the Seven Basic Elements in order for their positions to function effectively.

Vladimir Littauer described these key elements in *Commonsense Horsemanship*. The information was repeated in *Schooling and Riding the Sport Horse* by Paul Cronin. Following their teaching, I describe the Seven Basic Elements as follows:

The Seven Basic Elements of a functional position are:

1. CORRECT DESIGN OF POSITION

The rider sits close enough to the front of the saddle that the front of her breeches touches the pommel. She then tilts her hips and pelvis forward so as to bring her seat bones in contact with the saddle. Her chin is up so she can look between the horse's ears, and her shoulders are open.

The rider adjusts the stirrup length so the bottom of the stirrup iron is level with her ankle bone. (Stirrup length depends on the type of riding. This length is for the forward seat, cross-country and jumping.) She places the ball of her foot (not the toes) on the inside of the stirrup closest to the horse and allows her toes and knees to turn slightly out and her leg to be completely relaxed.

The rider's arms are softly flexed at the elbow, allowing her hands to be about ten inches apart and placed so there is a straight line from the bit to the elbow. The rider's hands and upper body move forward as the horse's speed increases or in jumping.

2. CORRECT DISTRIBUTION OF WEIGHT

When seated, the rider's weight is mostly in her seat bones. As the horse moves forward at faster gaits, when jumping or over uneven terrain, the rider allows the weight to flow evenly down her legs into the inside back of her heels. The amount of weight distributed from the seat to the heels should maintain a center line of gravity that corresponds with the horse's center of gravity.

3. BALANCE IN MOTION

The rider uses small, unconscious movements of her body, mostly her upper body, to maintain her stability on a moving horse *without gripping*.

4. Relaxation

The rider's muscles are soft and flexible, yet ready to quickly respond to the movements of the horse.

5. Rhythm

Once the rider has obtained a correct position, weight distribution, relaxation and balance, she unconsciously follows the cadence of the horse's movements with her body.

6. Spring

Once the rider has obtained a correct design of position, relaxation and weight distribution, the angles of her ankles, knees and hips will open and close absorbing the shock of the horse's movement.

7. Grip

Type 1 – Frictional grip – Frictional grip is the unconscious friction located where the rider's leg contacts the saddle (upper inner calf, inner knee and lower inner thigh). It is a result of correct design of position, relaxation and spring combined with the movement of the horse.

Type 2 – Muscular grip – The rider consciously contracts the muscles in the area where the rider's leg contacts the saddle (upper inner calf, inner knee and lower inner thigh). It is used only for a brief moment when the horse shies or bolts, perhaps in jumping, over uneven terrain or in reining patterns.

Though all styles and types of riding have their uses and merits, and I believe no style is overall superior to any other, I have found through my experience that certain styles lend themselves better to certain types of work. I would not try to rope and throw a steer in a jumping saddle, try to ride a cross country course balanced for Dressage or go fox hunting in a park saddle.

I have ridden many styles, including classical Forward Riding, classical Dressage, Western, Saddle Seat, racing and even cavalry using a military saddle. In doing so, I have found Sacred Connections Horsemanship is the most easily adaptable to a variety of other forms.

Because it incorporates techniques from Forward Riding, Sacred Connections Horsemanship helps the rider more swiftly and easily develop the Four Key Essentials and the Seven Basic Elements—*without hurting the horse*—than any other system I have studied. In addition to using Sacred Connections Horsemanship, for these exercises the rider should consider using a forward seat, all purpose saddle. Teaching the exercises to develop a functional position in other types of saddles is more difficult. Other types of saddles such as Western, Dressage or park saddles are not designed to ride in the forward balance position—standing in the stirrups or up off the horse's back, which more easily clears and opens the horse's chakras.

Once a rider develops a functional seat and begins to clear and connect with the horse's chakras using Sacred Connections Horsemanship, the rider can then adapt her seat for use in other styles of riding.

> Sacred Connections Horsemanship is probably the easiest and fastest way for a rider to achieve effective results *without hurting the horse*.

Defining the system:
In order to understand the rider's position from an energetic view, we should understand how the Seven Basic Elements help the rider achieve the Four Key Essentials. Though all seven elements are included in each of the Four Key

Essentials, some of the elements contribute more to certain essentials than others. The relationship between these factors is as follows:

1. UNITY OF THE HORSE AND RIDER IN MOTION ESPECIALLY REQUIRES:
Correct design of position
Correct distribution of weight
Balance in motion
Relaxation

2. SECURITY OF THE RIDER IN THE SADDLE ESPECIALLY REQUIRES:
Correct distribution of weight
Balance in motion
Spring
Grip

3. NON-ABUSE OF THE HORSE ESPECIALLY REQUIRES:
Correct distribution of weight
Spring
Relaxation

4. EFFECTIVE AIDS ESPECIALLY REQUIRE:
Correct design of position
Relaxation

We have discussed briefly how a nonfunctional position can prevent the horse from fully engaging all of his chakras. Now let us examine how the rider can ride in such a way as to maximize the opening and engagement of all the horse's chakras and connect fully to the Sacred.

Full engagement of the chakras manifests physically in the horse in one of three ways:

- Full collection, which Littauer termed "central balance."
- Semi-collection – central balance, but with less engagement of the hindquarters and less height of the steps. The head remains at the vertical and the horse is "through the back."
- Moving at high speed over uneven terrain and/or high jumping in a calm and natural state. Littauer defines this as "dynamic balance."

16. Though the horse's movement is highly animated in full collection, as shown here, his muscles are in a relaxed, rather than tense state, allowing him to engage all chakras.

In each type of movement, the horse fully engages the upper chakras and connects them to the lower chakras through the fourth chakra—the trust energy of the heart. The upper chakras—seventh, sixth and fifth—are considered to be in front of the girth area. The lower chakras—first, second and third—are considered to be behind the girth area. The fourth chakra acts as a bridge or connection between the upper and lower chakras. By connecting the upper and lower chakras through the positive energy of the fourth chakra, the horse transforms movement from the physical into sacred energy.

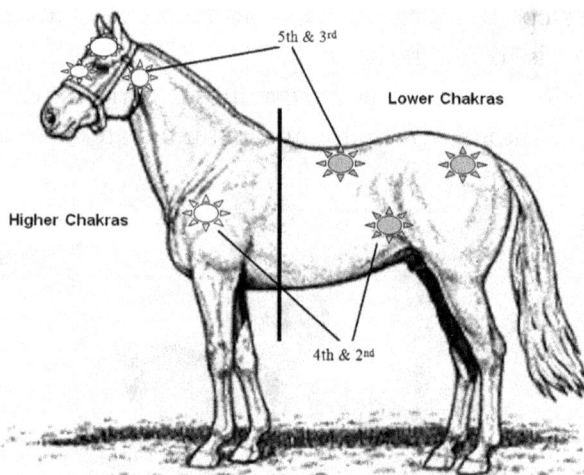

17. The fourth chakra, located in the heart area, acts as a bridge or connection between the upper and lower chakras.

In true central balance, semi-collection and moving in proper dynamic balance, the horse is relaxed and responsive to the rider's softest commands. Though the horse's movement is highly animated, the muscles are in a relaxed, rather than tense state. It is because the horse is physically relaxed and mentally engaged that he can respond to those softest of signals.

Although a frightened horse may display animated movement similar to that of collection or central balance, the horse is tense in his back, neck and jaw. He will resist the rider's commands, similar to a horse confused, scared or in pain as described in Chapter 4.

The physical dynamic of the horse in full collection manifests through the flow of energy from the horse's hindquarters. The rider asks for energy in the horse's hindquarters by using her legs to signal the horse to move forward. Once the energy flows through the first and second chakras, that area of the horse's body lowers and the energy moves upward.

For example, in full collection, the horse's croup area, that of the first and second chakras, lowers. The horse appears to be slightly "sitting" on his hindquarters.

*18. The lowering of the croup area, as seen in
full collection, is illustrated here. The horse
appears to be slightly "sitting" on his hindquarters.*

From the second chakra, the energy flows through the horse's third chakra and moves into the fourth and fifth chakras. The horse's croup area lowers, causing the angle of the sacrum to change (often called "lifting the back"). The horse's neck lifts and arches in preparation for the horse to flex in the jaw.

The rider now contains the energy with her hands and requires the horse to flex or give to the hands. The horse flexes in the fifth chakra, the throat area, willingly cooperating with the rider. The horse now begins to listen to the rider's guidance, bringing the energy into the sixth chakra, the horse's mind. The head and neck are raised, thus raising the fifth, sixth and seventh chakras.

> **When fully connecting to spirit, the horse moves his energy forward from the lower chakras to connect it with his higher chakras.**

If the rider continues to be soft and cooperative with the horse's efforts to transform the energy forward (impulsion), then the energy continues upward from the sixth chakra. The horse's poll is raised and the sixth chakra (the horse's face) becomes vertical. The seventh chakra is now the highest point on the horse's body and connects directly to the Sacred spirit.

From this place the energy flows back into the horse's body and through the chakras in a continuous circular pattern. The animation the horse shows is the constant flowing of sacred energy throughout the horse's system via the seventh chakra connection.

The same movement of energy can be seen in jumping where there is a moment of collection just before the horse leaves the ground. When the horse leaves the ground, he soars upward connecting into the seventh chakra (the poll), which continues to stretch out and forward as the horse arcs over the fence and lands on the ground.

In the dynamic balance employed when the horse travels at speed, over jumps or across uneven terrain, the horse transforms the energy in much the same way, but without the containment of energy requested by the rider's hands. Rather than requiring collection, the energy is pushed forward up the horse's spine and will connect with the Sacred during the changes in the horse's balance necessary for movement.

For example, when the horse transfers his weight to the hindquarters, engages his hocks and pushes forward, his head is up, connecting through the seventh chakra to the Sacred.

When the horse shifts his weight toward the forehand, allowing for the propulsion of the hindquarters, his head lowers. This circles the sacred energy back into the body, down the spine and through the chakras. Just as with the animated movement in full collection, the speed and excitement the horse and the rider feel when galloping is this constant pouring of sacred energy back into the horse's system.

> **In order for the horse to purely transmute the sacred energy through the chakras, his chakras must be clear and open.**

Transmuting sacred energy:
In order for the horse to purely transmute the sacred energy through the chakras, his chakras must be clear and open. As discussed in Chapter 1, it is not possible for the horse to clear and open his chakras when he experiences physical distractions such as pain or confusion created by a rider's non-functional seat. Any tension or resistance found in the horse's physical body will cause a block in the transmutation of energy and the flow will stop in that area of the horse's body.

There are several exercises that the rider can practice to open and clear the horse's chakras. These exercises described in the next chapter, physically manifest in the form of the Seven Basic Elements of a functional position. It is recommended that the rider practice on a quiet, schooled horse to gain a balanced, functional position.

Chapter 6
Practical Exercises to Develop a Chakra Rider

"So you teach Hunter/Jumper." Mary looked at me with wary skepticism in her intelligent, blue eyes.

I stared back, mirroring the same doubt and said, "So you teach Dressage." In my mind I pictured so many of today's self-acclaimed Dressage instructors teaching their students that collection comes from grabbing the reins and pulling the horse's nose into a "head-set."

I knew Mary was picturing today's typical "Hunt-Seat" counterpart—perching on the horse's withers and holding onto the reins for dear life while pounding the horse's back with an unsupported seat. Neither of us realized that moment of wariness was the beginning of a beautiful, life-long friendship.

Mary was a highly skilled classical Dressage rider and gifted instructor. At the time, I was unaware her experience trying to learn jumping was so bad that she had completely given up ever trying to ride over fences or cross-country. Yet she was brave enough to have me give her a sample lesson as part of an interview for a teaching job I wanted.

After Mary warmed up a quiet lesson horse, I complimented her position, then asked her to take the forward balance position we use for jumping. She easily trotted over the small jump and came back smiling. "That was the easiest jump I've ever been over."

Months later Mary confessed her earlier experience with jumping was disastrous. "I fell off every time," she said. "The instructor would tell me that happened in jumping and I just had to get over it. She was making me go over three-foot jumps and I couldn't stay on the horse."

Another time when Mary and I were teaching a clinic together, she pointed to a student practicing the forward balance position and said, "That's the same long, deep leg we use in Dressage. The stirrup is just shorter."

I smiled sagely, attempting to hide my excitement at her insight, and said, "Well of course it is. A good position is the same no matter how the rider and horse are balanced."

What Mary and I discovered and began mutually teaching was what Littauer was pointing out all along. It's not important how the position looks, but how it functions *with the horse*. Regardless of whether horses are being ridden Dressage, Forward Riding, Western or Saddle Seat, their basic structure and balance are the same. They may vary in conformation, size or build, may be gaited or not, but all horses have the same basic types of balance, move in similar ways and react with similar responses. The differences lie in the degree of agility, strength, knowledge and the type of balance they are using at the moment.

Consequently, the different types of riding, when done correctly, are about balance, rhythm, security, relaxation and communication, not about the rider keeping her heels down or head up. When instructors focus solely on details such as heels down or hands at a certain angle, students experience frustration similar to Mary's, attempting to contort their bodies into positions in which they can see no logic, connection or pattern. In addition, like Mary, they suffer from lack of security in the saddle that naturally produces a certain level of fear. What riders and instructors need to avoid the problems Mary and many others face is a simple, easy-to-follow, systematic approach to developing a functional position for both rider and horse.

Chapter 4 listed the Four Key Essentials necessary for a functional position in the saddle—any saddle. Chapter 5 broke these essentials down into basic elements a rider can identify and work with to develop a functional position. The following is a system of exercises that instructors and riders can use to create these elements.

EXERCISES TO DEVELOP A FUNCTIONAL POSITION

1. Forward balance position
2. Vertical far
3. Horizontal far
4. Back and shoulder curves
5. Ankle flexing

Exercise 1 – Forward balance position

A good place to begin is practicing in the forward balance position because the rider is standing in her stirrups rather than sitting on the horse's back. This helps clear and open the horse's lower chakras. Used correctly, the forward balance position is not only excellent for developing many of the Seven Basic Essentials, it is a wonderfully safe place for a rider to go when she is having trouble with her horse or riding over difficult terrain. No matter how strongly she grips with her legs, the rider can be bounced around or even off because, when gripping, she lacks a long deep leg and a solid foundation. Yet if she drops her weight into her heels and allows her legs to stay relaxed, she can absorb the shocks of the horse's movement in her ankles, knees and hips. In this position, she can ride out most bucks, rears, bolts and shies.

An excellent example of this security in the saddle happened when I was galloping racing Quarter Horses. I mounted one colt that was supposedly ready to be galloped. He immediately began to buck like an unbroken colt. Apparently, rather than gentling him to the saddle, his trainer had tried to break him by bucking him out the way cowboys use to bust broncs.

When the colt started to pitch, I simply stood up in the forward balance position and let him do his worst. When he couldn't buck me off, he actually threw himself to the ground—to the point of getting mud in his ear. (Of course this tactic did get me out of the saddle, but it also convinced the colt it wasn't worth the effort.)

The forward balance position is of course designed primarily for galloping and jumping. Used in slower gaits, it is an ideal exercise for developing correct weight distribution, balance in motion, spring, rhythm and frictional grip. It can also be used as a base for correct design of position.

Because the rider is up off the horse's back and uses the horse's mane to help her balance while learning, there is minimal risk of unintentionally hurting the horse.

The rider should practice the forward balance position in the ring at the walk, then at the trot, until she has enough balance and security to begin work over low jumps or uneven terrain. While in the forward balance position, the rider can feel the weight sliding down her legs into the heels and feel movement in the ankles, knees, hips and waist, which creates spring. This spring will help the rider acquire strength and balance without bouncing on the horse's back.

The forward balance position is generously used in developing position basics and clearing the horse's lower chakras. Once the rider obtains a functional seat, the forward balance position is reserved for riding at speed, over uneven terrain, over jumps and for schooling green horses. Most of the time the rider will be seated in the saddle when riding on the flat.

Developing the forward balance position

The rider should place herself as far forward in the saddle as possible without rising up on the pommel. She then grasps the horse's mane about halfway toward the horse's head and stands a couple of inches clear of the saddle. Her weight slides down the inside of the leg into the inside back of the heel.

The shoulders should incline forward enough to allow the elbows to bend somewhat. The rider's knees and hips should remain bent with the ankles in line with the hips. From the front the rider's toes appear to incline outward away from the horse. This allows for the weight to stay in the heels and spring to develop in the ankles. This will also place the correct part of the rider's leg—lower inner thigh, inner knee, upper inner calf—effortlessly against the saddle.

While learning the forward balance position, the rider should hold onto the horse's mane. This allows her to prevent herself from falling back onto the horse's back, or unintentionally pulling on a rein. She can also catch herself on the horse's neck if she loses her balance forward.

It is important to note that riding in the forward balance position removes our first and second chakras from the horse's self-confidence chakra until we have overcome our tension or fears and can comfortably balance while sitting on a moving horse.

The rider should start practicing the forward balance position at the walk with loose reins. Once she has gained her balance and rhythm at the walk, she can begin short trots, increasing the distance and adding turns as her balance increases.

19. Though originally designed primarily for galloping and jumping, practicing the forward balance position (shown here) is an ideal exercise for developing vital elements of a functional position.

NOTE: *The forward balance position differs from the "two point," or "half-seat" position, which has gained popularity in recent years. In the two-point position, the rider's toes point forward or slightly in toward the horse's elbow. She grips with her knees and her weight is somewhat on her knees and thighs rather than in her heels.*

Troubleshooting the forward balance position

Though the forward balance position is a very natural position for the rider and horse, there are some common misunderstandings that may arise as the rider attempts to find the correct design. Being aware of these misunderstandings helps the instructor, or the rider, either avoid them or easily identify and correct them.

Common challenges in developing the forward balance position

Problem:

Rider's feet are too far forward and the knees are straight:

This will cause the rider's balance to fall backward, and she will lose the spring in her knees. To correct, the rider should first sit back down in the saddle. Then she should move to the front of the saddle and retake the forward balance position by moving the hips forward rather than pushing them back.

20. If the rider's feet are too far forward and her knees are straight, she will lose the spring in her knees, lose her balance and tend to fall backward.

A good exercise to address this problem is called the "horizontal far." More information regarding the horizontal far can be found on page 88. The rider can try this exercise at walk and/or trot for short periods in this position as she is able.

Problem:

Rider's toes are turned in and she is gripping in the knee:
The rider should exaggerate turning out the knees and toes. The rider can also rise up on her toes for a moment, then turn her knees and toes way out and drop her weight into her heels. She will notice her heels sink deeper and the weight slides from the knees toward the heels.

21. If the rider's toes are turned straightforward or in, she will grip in her knee, preventing her weight from flowing to her heels.

Problem:

Back and shoulders are curved or rounded:
This is often a result of nervousness, tension and lack of core strength in the rider. It typically causes the rider's weight

to fall into the toes and removes the spring and the base of support in the heels. The rider should practice opening her shoulders, lifting her chest, relaxing her hips and waist and dropping her stomach toward the saddle.

22. Nervousness, tension and lack of core strength may cause the rider to curve her back and shoulders pushing her weight into her toes and removing the spring and the base of support in the heels.

Problem:

Rider is gripping in the knees or calves:

This will stiffen the rider's leg and prevent spring in the hip, knee and ankle. The weight will stop in the area that is gripping rather than sliding down the leg into the heel.

The rider should try to relax her leg using breathing and other relaxation techniques. The rider can also remove her feet from the stirrups and move her toes in circles. She can also use the vertical far and horizontal far at the trot.

Practicing the seated trot (without stirrups) is also helpful to relax a gripping leg. The rider must be certain to keep her legs loose. She should lean back somewhat and even hold the mane or the saddle until she has sufficient abdominal muscles with which to balance while sitting the trot in a more upright position.

> **NOTE:** *A beginner rider should only practice the sitting trot without stirrups for a short time on a quiet, stabilized horse in an enclosed area such as a small ring.*

Problem:
Rider's hands are too close to the saddle:

The rider's hands should be placed in a position to create a balanced triangle between the rider's hips, feet and hands (usually about one-third to halfway up the horse's neck, depending on the size of horse and rider).

23. While in the Forward Balance Position, the rider should place her hands about one-third to halfway up the horse's neck.

If the hands are too close to the saddle, the rider will be pushed too far back. If her hands are too far up the horse's neck the rider will have difficulty reaching and will feel over balanced to the front.

Problem:
Feet are placed on the outside of the stirrup:
It is important that the rider's feet are placed on the inside of the stirrup next to the horse and the stirrup is across the ball of her foot (at the joint just behind the toes).

Placing the foot on the inside of the stirrup helps prevent the toes from turning in and allows the rider's weight to slide to the inside back of the heel.

Problem:
The outside of the rider's ankle hurts:
The rider should check to be sure her toes are not turned in and the ankle is relaxed and flexing so the weight can slide to the *inside* back of the heel. The outside of the foot will be angled slightly up and out.

Exercise 2 – Vertical far
The vertical far is excellent for loosening the rider's back and gripping leg. The rider can also use this exercise if she is stiff in the hips, back or lower leg.

The best way to begin the vertical far is to shorten the stirrups two to three holes. The rider stands up in the stirrups and pushes her hips in front of the saddle and pulls her shoulders back behind her hips. The rider's back is bowed and her hips are in front of the saddle pommel.

The best way to balance in the vertical far is to push the hips in front of the shoulders. The rider can grab some mane near the saddle or, if she has very good hands, can ride on contact.

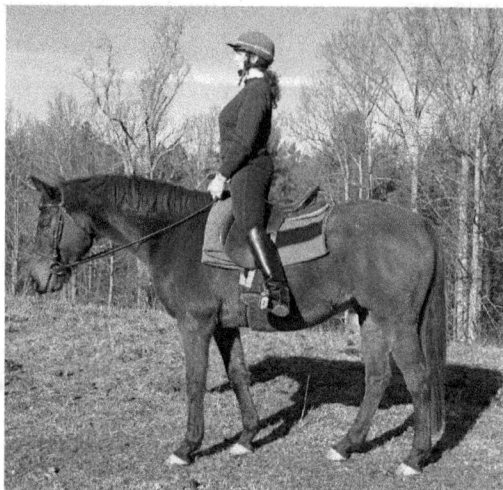

24. The vertical far is excellent for loosening the rider's back and hips as well as helping soften a gripping leg.

The rider should ride the vertical far at the walk and trot, switching back and forth from the vertical far to the forward balance position. As the rider improves she can use the vertical far at the canter, up and down hills and over fences. It is an excellent exercise to develop her balance in motion, correct weight distribution, spring and an overall athletic, well-balanced seat.

Exercise 3 – Horizontal far

The horizontal far is excellent for loosening the back, especially the shoulders, developing a long, deep leg and loosening a gripping thigh and calf. It will help open a stiff hip and teach the rider's hips to have more spring. The horizontal far works well for a rider who tends to push her leg forward and her hips back. It is also an excellent tool for teaching the rider to feel the movement of the horse's head and neck at the canter.

*25. The horizontal far is good for a rider who tends
to push her leg forward and her hips back.*

The rider takes a forward balance position, then stretches her arms and upper body forward and grabs mane at the horse's poll. It is extremely important that the rider maintain the weight in her heels while practicing this exercise. She should practice this exercise at the walk and trot, frequently changing from the horizontal far to the forward balance position and back.

Exercise 4 – Back and shoulder curves

Curving the back and shoulders will help the rider loosen a stiff back and open rounded shoulders.

The rider obtains the forward balance position, then tucks her head, rounds her shoulders and back and pulls her stomach up and away from the saddle. The rider will naturally rise up on her toes in the stirrups as high as possible. She holds this position for a few seconds, then raises her head and opens her back and shoulders. She should arch her back and drop her stomach toward the saddle. The rider will usually feel her weight drop back into her heels as the back and shoulders open.

NOTE: *This exercise is usually only practiced at the halt and the walk as it is virtually impossible for a rider to maintain weight in her heels while her shoulders are rounded and back curved.*

26. *Curving the back and shoulders will help the rider loosen a stiff back and open rounded shoulders.*

Exercise 5 – Ankle flexing

This exercise is excellent for the rider with gripping calves or stiff ankles. It assists her in getting more depth and weight into the heels and helps create spring in the ankle. Because the rider is not secure in the saddle while practicing this exercise, it is usually only practiced at the walk.

The rider obtains the forward balance position, then stands up on her toes as far as possible. She holds this position for a few seconds, then sinks deeply down into her heels and bends her knees and ankles. This exercise should be repeated several times throughout the session until she is feeling more depth in her heels and looseness in her calves and ankles.

While practicing these exercises, it is important to observe the horse's reactions to the rider's various movements and releases of tension. An observant rider will be able to feel or see when the horse reacts favorably, thus letting her know she has given the horse the freedom to open his chakras.

Once the rider has developed a secure, functional position, she can begin a program of using that position to clear and open the horse's chakras.

Chapter 7
A Program Guide
for Opening the Chakras

"MY HORSE WON'T TURN," COMPLAINED TRACY, WHO was retraining an 18-year-old Morgan. "He puts his head down and acts like he wants to buck or else he pulls and goes the other way."

Tracy's rescued horse was recovering and rebuilding muscle from several years of injuries, neurological problems, malnutrition, unbalanced shoeing and uneducated riders.

"What size turns are you trying?" I asked her.

"About this big," she said, while demonstrating a small circle about ten meters in diameter.

"Your horse doesn't have the muscle and agility to make that small a turn while carrying a rider," I explained.

I suggested she start with large, twenty- to thirty-meter circles at the walk as well as walking up and down low hills for a couple of weeks. We also added walking the horse over some ground poles and slightly raised poles (six inches) to get him to begin using his back and hindquarters.

The next week Tracy came and gave me a big hug. "Thank you!" she said, grinning. "My horse will turn! I didn't realize I was hurting him with those tight turns."

Tracy is an example of so many riders today who are not aware they are asking too much of their horse too soon. Today's riders see advanced riding at shows, on ESPN and in magazines and aspire to these measures of riding skill.

In their efforts to "properly" ride and/or train their horses, many riders ask for fairly advanced moves—such as flexing in the jaw, turning on the forehand or hindquarters, canter lead changes, cantering from a halt or going on the bit— before the horse has the muscles to balance a rider through such moves.

Though it is admirable for riders to set such quality performances as their goals, many riders are unaware of the hard work, long hours and level of skill involved in reaching such goals. In our "I want it now" society, today's riders often buy into the commercialism and showmanship that have many believing an inexperienced rider can break and train a horse in a few weeks or months. In reality, it takes years to fully develop a horse or rider to such levels as Grand Prix Dressage, high jumping or advanced reining patterns.

German Bereiter and Founding member of Xenophon, Dr. Gerd Heuschmann, stated in his book, *Tug of War – Classical Versus "Modern" Dressage:* "No athlete is able to perform to his utmost, peak at the right moment and remain healthy without having built up his body (and mind) over a significant period of time."

Heuschmann continues: "It takes time and a great deal of patience to train a horse until it's ready to compete while at the same time, maintaining its physical and mental health– and to keep it fit until old age."

Unfortunately, the horses are often the ones that suffer. When a well-intentioned, yet not-thoroughly-trained rider attempts to put a horse on the bit or asks for collection too early in the horse's training, the horse has neither the physical strength nor the mental or emotional capacity to respond correctly. Just as with Tracy's horse, such mounts wind up stiff and confused, resisting the rider's efforts and/or falling prey to harsh bits, tie downs and frustrated riders. The horses stay stuck in their first and second chakras, and the riders are robbed of the reward of a satisfying ride, much less finding a true connection with their horses.

By using a systematic program of schooling properly designed to accommodate the horse's physical, mental and emotional abilities and needs, a capable rider can make meaningful connections with her horse throughout all levels of training. As the horse advances through the chakras, the rider will be able to sustain those connections for longer periods of time.

An effective training program can take as much as a year or more before the rider connects consistently with the horse's higher chakras. Of course this time frame depends on the level and abilities of the horse and the rider. This program also assumes the horse is sound, already accepting a saddle and rider and responsive to simple signals.

The rider should allow for more than a year, preferably two, for horses not yet broken to ride. Horses with problems may take longer as they will need to be rehabilitated and/or retrained.

If the rider wishes to ride consistently in full collection using seventh chakra energy, then she should be prepared to train her horse for at least two or more years. This is because it takes time to build the horse's strength to perform at full collection while carrying a rider.

This program also assumes the rider has some experience and a fairly stable position. Obviously the more experienced and capable the rider, the more effective she will be in the training. As always it is best for beginning riders to first learn their balance and basics on a schooled horse with a qualified trainer.

A clear, step-by-step system helps the rider assess the horse's current status and determine when the horse is ready to move on to the next level or exercise. The program of clearing and opening the chakras is similar to Littauer's program of schooling outlined in *Common Sense Horsemanship*.

The rider should begin with an assessment of the horse's physical, mental and emotional status. It is important for her to understand which chakra energy the horse is engaging.

> **Many times during training, the rider will be able to establish a divine connection with her horse before they reach advanced level riding.**

The first three to five months of this training program are about opening and clearing the horse's chakras. It also includes connecting with the horse's first three chakras, thus creating a healthy self-confidence in the horse. Just as a human with healthy self-confidence has released her fears and ego, a horse with healthy self-confidence has released his fears, can respond quietly to the rider's simple commands, goes calmly on loose reins and is willing and cooperative. A horse with a strong sense of self-confidence is ready to trust his rider to make the decisions about where and how fast he will go and in what way he will travel. At this level the horse is ready to begin balancing and moving softly on contact.

This opening and clearing of the chakras in the first three to five months of schooling is accomplished by using voice

commands and stabilization—maintaining even speeds—
described in Chapters 11 & 13. By first teaching the horse
voice commands and stabilization, the rider can develop
the trust necessary for the horse to move into the higher
chakras. Teaching him stabilization and voice commands
greatly reduces the amount of pressure from the hands or
legs required for control. Voice commands also help avoid
any physical threat the horse may associate with the rider.

Similar to working freely on the ground, stabilization, voice
commands and loose reins allow the horse to relax and *choose*
to respond to the rider. This choice immediately brings the
relationship of the horse and rider into higher (fourth and
fifth) chakra energies.

The rider will have access to the horse's higher chakras once
he has gained enough confidence to begin trusting her. The
horse can now physically, mentally and emotionally handle
longer more detailed training sessions and is now ready to
begin thinking about his responses. This allows for a better
quality of communication between the horse and rider and a
higher level of performance.

> **The rider should allow more than a
> year, preferably two, for training
> horses not yet broken to ride.**

The relationship between this training program and the
flow of chakra energy is:

FIRST MONTH – FIRST AND SECOND CHAKRA

THE RIDER:
- Makes the horse feel safe
- Provides adequate nutrition

- Removes all sources of pain
- Removes all threats perceived by the horse
- Establishes who is leader when on the ground
- Establishes healthy boundaries
- Establishes rules the horse can clearly understand and easily follow

THE RIDER USES THE FOLLOWING TOOLS TO ACCOMPLISH THE ABOVE LISTED ACHIEVEMENTS:

- Lunging
- Stabilization
- Voice Commands
- Correction
- Reward
- Quality nutrition
- Quality hoof care and dental work
- A calm, relaxed, safe environment
- Properly fitting equipment
- Adequate turnout

SECOND MONTH – SECOND CHAKRA

THE RIDER:

- Establishes a one to one relationship with the horse from the saddle
- Establishes herself as leader when riding
- Develops the horse's physical ability to balance the rider
- Develops the horse's ability to understand and respond to simple commands

THE RIDER USES THE FOLLOWING TOOLS TO ACCOMPLISH THE ABOVE LISTED ACHIEVEMENTS:

- Riding at the walk and trot
- A forward balance or non-interfering position

- Loose or long reins
- Simple turns at walk and trot
- Simple rein and leg signals
- Voice commands
- Reward and correction

THIRD THROUGH FIFTH MONTHS – THIRD CHAKRA

THE RIDER:
- Develops the horse's agility
- Develops the horse's self confidence

THE RIDER USES THE FOLLOWING TOOLS TO ACCOMPLISH THE ABOVE LISTED ACHIEVEMENTS:
- Loose or long reins
- Combinations of simple leg and rein signals
- Lateral agility exercises
- Longitudinal agility exercises
- Hill work
- Riding at the canter
- Low/simple jumping

NEXT THREE TO SIX MONTHS – FOURTH CHAKRA

THE RIDER:
- Establishes trust in the horse
- Develops a soft and more precise control of the horse
- Increases the quality of communication between horse and rider

THE RIDER USES THE FOLLOWING TOOLS TO ACCOMPLISH THE ABOVE LISTED ACHIEVEMENTS:
- Riding on soft contact
- Using hands and legs in cooperation with each other and at times with the horse's movement

- Sitting at all gaits when on flat ground
- More advanced leg and rein signals used in combinations
- Riding in company of other horses

NEXT SIX MONTHS TO TWO YEARS – FIFTH AND SIXTH CHAKRAS

THE RIDER:
- Develops a higher quality and greater quantity of strength and agility in the horse
- Establishes full cooperation between horse and rider
- Teaches the horse more complicated maneuvers
- Increases quality of communication
- Increases quality of performance

THE RIDER USES THE FOLLOWING TOOLS TO ACCOMPLISH THE ABOVE LISTED ACHIEVEMENTS:
- Riding "on the bit"
- Flexions
- Higher jumping
- Smaller circles and turns at trot and canter
- Using hands and legs in full cooperation with the horse
- Riding at speed
- Riding over uneven terrain

AFTER ONE TO TWO YEARS – SEVENTH CHAKRA

THE RIDER:
- Communicates with the horse primarily through energetic connections
- Develops an extremely high quality of performance
- Establishes a continuous flow of energy between horse and rider

THE RIDER USES THE FOLLOWING TOOLS TO ACCOMPLISH THE ABOVE LISTED ACHIEVEMENTS:

- Semi- and full collection
- High jumping
- Speed
- High jumping at speed
- Agility exercises while on the bit or in semi- or full collection

Of course some horses will take longer to advance through certain stages of training while others may work through rather quickly. It is important for the rider to recognize the signs of a horse who is ready to move on to the next lesson or level:

1) so the horse does not become bored and
2) so the horse is not advanced more rapidly than he is ready.

Chapters 8 and 9 give a more detailed description of the exercises best used during each month of schooling as well as descriptions showing when a horse is ready to move forward.

The rider must keep in mind that training is as much about the horse's body as it is his mind and emotions. In addition to learning to understand and trust the rider, he *must* be given time to develop the physical ability to perform with a rider on his back.

If for any reason the horse's training is interrupted for more than a few weeks, the rider must be certain to reassess what the horse has retained mentally and emotionally. She may need to go back and review a few lessons. In this system however, unlike many methods, unless a rider violates the horse's trust, he typically retains most of his training.

One area the rider must rebuild is the horse's physical condition. If the rider has worked the horse up to the fourth or fifth month, then stops the training for three months, she will need to go back to the second-and-third-month work for a short time. This allows the horse to stretch and re-tone unused muscles. Of course she will not have to spend as much time schooling the horse, which will reduce the time needed for these exercises compared to when training first began. In such a case, the rider can use more work over uneven terrain to build such muscles since the horse is already trained for riding outside the ring.

Chapter 8
Baby Steps – The First Three Chakras

"**E**ITHER YOUR MULE GETS TRAINED OR YOU HAVE TO move him. He's dangerously out of control," I had to tell Melinda shortly after she brought her 15-year-old mule to board at my barn. Jake had nearly run several people over trying to either get to food or simply run away in fear. He ran through gates at least once or twice a week, tried to bite several times and one of his kicks actually bruised a woman's ribs.

Melinda had purchased Jake from a less than reputable trail barn where he was being used for rental trail rides. She tried several systems of training before she came to my barn, all with little to no success. She didn't admit it at the time, but she was very scared to ride Jake.

"Show me," she said. "I've tried everything. I don't know what else to do. I work him and work him to get him to submit, and he just has these meltdowns where he panics and runs away. When he does that, he's out of control."

Prior to our conversation, I had watched Jake when Debbie, a member of my barn staff, was leading him out to the field. Jake was pulling on the lead rope, dragging Debbie around and not paying any attention. When I asked her to stop a moment, Jake wouldn't stand still. He pulled and dragged on the lead rope, fidgeted and tried to bite the handler.

I walked over and took the lead rope, gave Jake a couple of sharp tugs and firmly said, "Stand!"

He stood for a brief moment, then started to fidget again. I repeated the sharp tugs and the verbal command. After three tries Jake finally stood still for about fifteen seconds. When I reached up to stroke his neck and praise him, I realized he was shaking in fear.

I shared this insight with Melinda. "He's scared because he doesn't know what you want of him. Jake doesn't know the rules and how to please you."

I went on to explain to Melinda why working horses (or mules) over and over confuses them and places them in freeze mode. I pointed out that mules and horses do not deal well with confusion, inconsistency and unclear signals and explained that Jake not only did not understand, but constantly felt threatened when she worked him in circles to try and get him to submit.

Bless her heart, Melinda started to cry. Like so many well-intentioned horse owners, she didn't realize the effect she was having on her equine. "It makes perfect sense when you think about it," she said. "Poor Jake! No wonder he had so many meltdowns."

We began Jake on a program to open and clear his chakras and rebuild the trust he had lost. Melinda was incredible. She read Littauer, sat through theory classes and took notes, and worked very hard to be clear and consistent when she handled Jake. Most important, Melinda *stuck to the program*.

She never rushed Jake, changed the way she handled him or lost patience.

After a few weeks Jake no longer tried to kick, bite or run people over. He stopped breaking through gates and would stand quietly when being handled. Melinda no longer had to spend twenty to thirty minutes chasing him in the field to catch him. When Jake saw her car on the road he would head to the gate and wait for her.

Today Melinda can ride her mule without a bridle or halter and he is being used for beginner lessons. Melinda is ecstatic and thrilled. "You told me," she said. "I didn't believe it was possible, but I can do anything with him now."

Unfortunately Jake's past experience is more common than not. I think many owners are as confused as their horses when it comes to training. There are so many ideas, theories and experts telling them what to do, they wind up in circles, their horses even more upset and confused.

Yet Melinda and Jake, along with so many others, are proof the Sacred Connections Horsemanship system works—if the rider works the system. By understanding how each stage builds on the one before, by sticking to the system, following through with details and consistency and not rushing their horse before he is ready, more horse (and mule) owners can have quiet, happy, cooperative equines that meet them at the gate to be ridden.

First month: Ground work and Lunging

FIRST AND SECOND CHAKRAS

GOAL – Address the survival and pecking order issues by providing leadership, furnishing adequate nutrition, stabling the horse in a safe environment and assuring the horse is pain free.

The rider or trainer must first be certain the horse is not in pain and has his nutritional needs adequately satisfied. As we discovered in Chapter 2, a horse who is constantly craving minerals or other proper nutrition simply cannot understand or even pay attention to what the rider is attempting to ask of him.

The same is true for a horse who is sore anywhere in his body, including his back, shoulders, hips or feet. A sore horse will immediately associate his pain with the rider and will be unable to trust her. Chapter 14 includes more information on proper nutrition and identification of possible causes of pain.

If the rider begins the training by setting healthy boundaries, the horse will know how he is expected to behave. Just as the individual horse wants to know his status and behavior in the herd, the horse being ridden or trained wants to clearly know where he stands with the rider.

I recall a teenage student who owned a lovely, but nervous and often jumpy Quarter Horse named Dancer. When Cindy would try to lead Dancer from the ground, the horse was always pulling on the lead rope to try and eat grass, turning his head to see where the other horses were, wandering away from the direction Cindy was headed and spooking and jumping at things as simple as grass or paper blowing by. Dancer's behavior bled over into their riding as the horse was always rushing at every gait and Cindy felt forced to use a severe bit to control him.

As I watched Cindy leading Dancer, I realized she didn't pay attention to or engage the horse. Cindy was either talking on her cell phone, talking with her friends, watching other horses or riders or doing various other things that robbed her attention. By the time Cindy realized Dancer was distracted or spooking, they were already in a dangerous or difficult situation.

With a capable horse handler, the horse's main focus will remain on the handler, rather than on other horses or events nearby. If the horse's attention drifts the slightest bit, the handler will quite subtly and quickly bring the horse's attention back to her, usually by a soft and subtle tug on the lead shank or touch on the shoulder. This occurs long before the horse's attention is completely distracted, resulting in the horse feeling the handler is in control of the situation and looking out for the horse's safety. In the horse's mind, the handler is aware enough to see "danger" coming before it gets too close.

Healthy boundaries include such things as not allowing the horse to bite, kick or walk on top of his handler. The horse is expected to walk quietly on a lead next to the handler's shoulder. He must wait to be asked to move through gates and should halt easily and softly when asked. The horse should not be allowed to nibble or ask for a treat.

NOTE: *I use treats a great deal in the first stages of training. They help the horse feel safe because he is being given sustenance (first chakra) and this establishes a relationship of safety between the horse and rider (second chakra). The horse will also clearly understand when he has done what is asked. Chapter 13 includes more information regarding the proper use of treats as reward.*

If the rider or handler does not allow the horse to look for a treat, i.e. nibble at hands or pockets, then the horse usually does not learn to bite. The handler must also be careful to not play with or tease the horse's mouth and nose area. This is another important factor in establishing healthy boundaries.

It can take four to six weeks to make healthy boundaries an integral part of a horse's daily behavior. For these early weeks of training, the handler/rider may feel as if she is nit-picking or correcting the horse for nearly every little thing. However, the rider should not despair or reduce her vigilance. Horses that have been spoiled or confused will often "test" their handlers or easily fall into old habits.

> While treats are an excellent form of reward in early stages of training, the horse must not be allowed to ask for treats or nibble as this can encourage biting.

By being very clear, fair and consistent with her correction and very lavish with reward, the handler will develop a horse who is not only safer to handle from the ground, but safer to ride because he will first, above all else, listen to the rider. The horse will feel safe around the handler/rider and will therefore pay more attention to the rider and feel safe cooperating with her commands. This is first and second chakra energy.

LUNGING:

Any effective schooling program will begin by first establishing healthy boundaries between the horse and rider. When used correctly lunging is a great tool for teaching respect, healthy boundaries, voice commands and stabilization. It is important not to work the horse too long on the lunge line, so he is not injured or soured. A good lunging session should last approximately ten to twenty minutes.

For more information on lunging see Littauer's *Common Sense Horsemanship* and Jane Marshall Dillon's *School for Young Riders* or a good text specifically on lunging.

NOTE: *In this program, lunging is never used to "tire" the horse or to "get the bucks out." It is used to teach the horse voice commands and rhythm so running away and bucking do not become problems.*

Once the horse is stabilized at the walk, trot and halt on the lunge line in both directions, the handler should teach the horse to lunge at three speeds both at the walk and the trot, i.e. the medium walk, the fast walk and the slow walk and the medium trot, the fast trot and the slow trot.

The horse should quickly shift into the desired speed upon the voiced command of the handler, such as "walk out" for a fast walk or "slow" for a slower speed within the gait. The horse should then continue at that speed until the handler tells him to change. Chapter 11 contains more information on the use of voice commands.

SIGNS THE HORSE IS READY TO MOVE BEYOND LUNGING:
- The horse responds quickly and willingly to voice commands while on the lunge line.
- The horse is stabilized at three speeds of the walk and trot going both directions on the lunge line.
- The horse will stand quietly at the halt for several seconds.
- The horse is respectful and cooperative to the rider's signals while being handled and led.
- The horse appears to be growing bored with the repetition of lunging.

Second month: Riding at the Walk and Trot

SECOND CHAKRA

GOAL - The rider develops leadership from the saddle using clear, consistent boundaries and communication.

The rider rides the horse at the walk while sitting quietly in the saddle and using loose reins and voice commands. She should ride at the walk also in the forward balance position interspersed with time sitting in the saddle. If the horse speeds up, the rider should first use voice then, only if necessary, a soft check-release of the reins, described in Chapter 11, to slow the horse down. The rider should ride at the walk for the first two or three sessions of no more than ten to twenty minutes.

During the first few rides, the rider should ask for simple halts with the voice and make two or three large circles of at least twenty to thirty meters. These circles should be done primarily with the rider in the forward balance position or at least leaning forward, which allows the horse to stretch and build his muscles. She should reward the horse lavishly, with a treat or pats when he responds favorably, and correct the horse justifiably with a check-release when he does not cooperate, as discussed in Chapter 13.

At this stage the rider uses the leading rein described in Chapter 11 for *all* turns. The rider should *not* use a leg for turns at this stage. The horse is learning or relearning to balance a rider with open chakras and developing muscles not used before.

> Asking a horse to engage his hindquarters before he is physically capable of doing so with a rider can negatively impact his self-confidence (third chakra).

Adding leg in a turn asks the horse to balance more on his hindquarters or "engage" them while attempting to balance the rider in a turn. This can be beyond the capability of a green horse and stresses either undeveloped or poorly developed muscles. Especially in the case of a horse with a sore back or emotional issues, asking a horse to balance on the hindquarters before he has the muscles or the emotional ability to do so in a *calm and relaxed* manner can violate his trust. This causes the horse to stiffen through the first, second and third chakras and close down his fourth chakra.

Though he may try, a green horse in the early stages of training is not physically or mentally capable of shifting his weight toward the hindquarters and fully engaging his hindquarters, while carrying a rider. Attempting this level of riding a green horse can negatively impact the his self-confidence (third chakra) because he is not capable of performing what the rider asks.

During this early stage of riding, the horse will be clearing and opening his second chakra and will carry his head and neck slightly lower than the withers. This is perfectly normal because the horse is attempting to balance with the weight of the rider and is shifting that weight away from the second chakra area. The horse is also stretching forward in his thoracic area, clearing and opening a space into which the energy created in the first two chakras can move.

As the horse learns to manage the first and second chakra energy and builds strength in his core, he will naturally return his head and neck to a more normal position.

The rider can help the horse with this forward movement of energy by staying forward when sitting in the saddle and riding much of this stage in the forward balance position. This removes both the rider's weight and root chakra from the horse's first three chakras and opens the space for the forward thrust of energy.

NOTE OF CAUTION: *Many trainers use the recently popular method of getting a horse to "disengage the hindquarters," in an attempt to supple the horse. From the ground, the trainer uses a whip or a stick to push the hindquarters away while pulling the horse's head toward her.*

In her book Horse Gaits, Balance and Movement, *Susan E. Harris addresses this and other attempts to supple a horse by pushing his hindquarters one way and turning his head another. On page 95, Harris states, "Some riders and trainers confuse bending with neck flexibility." She goes on to say that a truly supple horse's ability to bend "comes more from the engagement of his inside hind leg and the lifting of his back than from bending his neck. Misguided attempts to supple a horse by pulling his mouth from side to side . . . are more likely to produce sore muscles, resistance and evasions like rubbernecking than true suppleness and balance in turns."*

Harris states on page 75, "Trying to create a certain mode of balance by forcing the head to do this, the hocks to do that, while the shoulders do something else, misses the point: good movement comes from good balance along with other essential gait qualities, not from putting the pieces together."

Horses that have had back problems or have experienced riders with very heavy hands will especially, once given a loose rein, lower their heads and stretch the neck and back. Often these horses will travel several strides with their noses almost on the ground.

*28. In the first stages of mounted work, the horse
will often carry his head below the shoulder.*

As long as the horse is going quietly and safely, the rider should allow him this extreme stretching. The horse is not only trying to undo years of sore and cramped muscles, he is trying to discover to what extent he can move his head. Since the horse uses his head and neck for balance, a formerly abused horse will extend his head and neck as far as he can to see what kind of room he has.

> Once on a loose rein, horses that have had
> back problems or have experienced riders with
> very heavy hands will travel several strides
> with their noses almost on the ground.

This is a test for the fourth chakra because the horse is finding out if he can trust the rider to allow him the space he needs to balance. A horse who feels he has free use of his head and neck for balance will feel safer (second chakra) and become bolder in his movement (third chakra – self-confidence).

> **A horse who has free use of his head and neck for balance is safer to ride and is able to produce freer movement.**

SIGNS THE HORSE IS READY TO TROT WITH THE RIDER:

- The horse is quietly stabilized at the walk and halt, with the rider both sitting in the saddle and in the forward balance position.
- The horse maintains the same rhythm and relaxation when the rider asks him to turn.
- The horse appears to be getting a little bored with the repetition of walking.

The rider now begins trotting the horse a few times during each session, which should last approximately twenty minutes. At this stage, the rider uses a forward balance position while trotting along the rail and begins to add large circles and turns.

After the horse is going quietly at the trot, the rider begins posting for short stretches while in the forward balance position. This stage will continue for a month or two, depending on the horse's and rider's experience and ability.

In **posting while in the forward balance position**, the rider does not sit down in the saddle but simply bends the knee and hip slightly. This allows her to softly catch the rhythm of posting without actually sitting on the horse's back.

The purpose of this type of posting is to make the horse aware of the rhythm. A rider can speed a horse up or slow him down by changing the rhythm of her posting. Posting at this stage from the forward balance position can also ease any stress on the rider's back.

By the time the horse is ready to begin cantering, the rider can switch from posting in the forward balance position to posting from the saddle. This type of posting will correspond with the exercises used to prepare the horse for work on contact.

Third through Fifth months: Beginning Agility
THIRD CHAKRA

GOAL – Develop self-confidence in the horse through strength and agility.

In the third month the rider should see the horse carry his head slightly higher than he has before. This means the horse is starting to develop the strength to more easily balance a rider. The horse will also not be so inclined to stretch his neck out and down in the turns as he may have before. The horse is now ready for more and smaller turns and different speeds at the gaits.

SIGNS THE HORSE IS READY TO BEGIN SIMPLE AGILITY WORK:
- The horse is well stabilized at the walk, trot and halt.
- The horse is easily handling large circles at the walk and trot with the rider in the forward balance position.
- The horse will stand quietly at the halt for several seconds.
- The horse is beginning to carry his head slightly higher.
- The horse appears to be getting a little bored with the repetition of walking and trotting.

TURNS:
The horse can now handle smaller, more frequent turns such as ten-to-twenty-meter circles. Other good exercises are large serpentines and squared turns.

For **squared turns** the rider guides the horse along the railing for approximately one stride. The rider then turns the horse toward the center of the ring for approximately one stride and then turns the horse parallel to the railing for one stride, then back to the railing. Once the horse reaches the railing, the rider turns him in the original direction he was going along the railing. The corners of each turn should be right angles, and the lines should be straight. The turns look similar to connected boxes opened at one end.

28. An illustration of the squared turns which are an ideal exercise to help the horse develop lateral agility.

At this stage the rider should add a tap of the outside heel in the turns. She should still be using her forward balance position and leading reins for these turns. By adding a tap with the outside heel, the rider introduces the horse to pushing more strongly with the outside hind leg. This will move the horse forward and ask him to begin engaging his hindquarters in turns.

By staying in the forward balance position, the rider allows the horse freer use of his hindquarters and back without the interfering weight of the rider. The horse once again learns he can trust the rider not to interfere and can begin to increase the engagement of his hindquarters and use the proper muscles.

JUMPING:

The horse should begin low jumping in the third month (if he is at least four years old, or five years if he is a Warmblood or Arabian.) Low jumping will strengthen the horse's back and increase his longitudinal agility.

29. By the third month of schooling, the horse is ready for low jumping which will increase the horse's longitudinal agility.

SIGNS THE HORSE IS READY TO BEGIN JUMPING:

- The horse is stabilized at the walk and trot on loose reins.
- The horse is responding well to the rider's voice commands.
- The horse appears to be getting a little bored with the repetition of trotting.

The rider should begin with five to six ground poles, also called cavaletti poles, spaced about four feet apart. If the horse has never been through ground poles before, the rider should walk him through a few times giving him the space to drop his nose down and look at or sniff the poles. The rider should keep the horse fairly straight and not allow him to speed up, stop or turn out of the poles.

Once the horse walks quietly through the poles, the rider can begin trotting through them. *Common Sense Horsemanship* contains more information on schooling over cavaletti poles and jumps.

The rider should use her forward balance position and loose reins through the poles and over low jumps. Even the most accomplished rider should grab mane over a jump when riding a green horse as the rider can never be certain what the horse may do. This prevents the possibility of the rider falling back and hitting the horse in the back with her seat. It is better to grab mane in training than to risk violating the horse's trust.

The rider can work the horse at the trot over low jumps, i.e. one foot gradually increasing to two feet. The horse should be jumped occasionally during schooling (about every third or fourth session). The jumps may be varied by using small spreads and moving on to low in and outs and low bounces (no strides).

Increases in the jumping should be done gradually so as not to mentally or physically overface the horse. The horse should jump quietly on loose reins and remain stabilized on the approach as well as on the landing after two or three canter strides. At this level, approaches to the jump should be at the trot.

The jumping engages the first, second and third chakras, helping build and strengthen these areas as the horse develops confidence and trust in the rider. It is essential that the rider have a solid position in order not to grip the horse's sides, fall back and hit the horse in the back or jerk the horse in the mouth.

HILLS:

Along with jumping, it is time to begin working the horse outside the ring over uneven terrain and up and down hills. Hill work will also help the horse's longitudinal agility and strength in the core and hindquarters (first, second and third chakras) for jumping and carrying the rider.

SIGNS THE HORSE IS READY TO WORK OUTSIDE A RING

- The horse is quietly stabilized at the walk, trot and halt on loose reins.
- The horse responds well to voice commands.
- The horse is calm and rhythmical while performing circles and turns
- The horse appears to be getting a little bored with repetitive ring work.

The rider begins in the corner of a small field and uses the fence as if it were two sides of the ring railing. Using the imagination, she visualizes a line that can serve as the other two "sides" of the imaginary ring.

The rider repeats the same exercises she practiced in the ring, beginning with a quiet walk on loose reins; including halts, stabilized trotting at a medium speed, circles and turns.

She can gradually increase the area until riding along the fence of the entire field. This is done over the course of several sessions.

If the horse is responding quietly and stabilized on loose reins (horses' gaits are naturally bigger and slightly faster in the open than in a ring), he can begin hill work.

The rider should always ride up *and down* hills in a forward balance position, or in a vertical far or horizontal far, in order to stay balanced with the horse. The section on balance in Chapter 12 contains more information about why the rider does *not* lean back going down hills.

Hill work begins with a small incline at a walk. If the horse is going quietly on loose reins at a stabilized walk, the rider can begin trotting up the hill. If the horse handles this quietly, she can continue trotting up and down the hill.

The rider must be aware of the horse's breathing to be certain she does not overwork him and stress his wind. A good gauge to assess his breathing is to go up and down the hill two to three times, walk the horse on flat ground for a minute or two, then halt the horse and look at his belly and nostrils to see how fast he's breathing. If fast, the rider should continue walking the horse on flat ground to let him catch his breath.

After repeating this two to three times in the first session, the rider can gradually increase the number of times she rides the horse up and down the hill over several sessions of hill work, then move on to a steeper hill. These sessions should be interspersed with ring work and jumping so as not to sour the horse on any one type of work.

CANTERING:

The horse can now balance a rider at the canter even in the confines of a ring. The rider begins by allowing the horse to canter a few strides longer after a jump before asking the horse to come back to a trot.

Next the rider can signal for a canter from the trot, asking for a canter while in the forward balance position and in a corner of the ring to encourage the proper canter lead. The rider can canter the horse a time or two around the ring, keeping the horse on loose reins and quietly stabilized at an even speed. This exercise should be repeated in both directions and about every third time the horse is ridden.

The horse should now have enough strength to balance the rider comfortably on loose or long reins through the walk, trot and canter, over low combinations of jumps and up and down hills. This strength will directly reflect in the horse's self-confidence (third chakra).

A horse with healthy self-confidence responds quietly to the rider's simple signals, goes quietly on loose reins and is willing. A horse with a strong sense of self-confidence is ready to trust his rider (fourth chakra) to make the decisions about where he will go, what his speed will be and in what manner he will travel. The horse is now capable of balancing and moving softly on contact.

Part III

Empowering Partnership

Chapter 9
Working in the Higher Chakras

I AM AMAZED THAT WARLORD EVER LET ANYONE RIDE him. A big-hearted, 16.2 hand Thoroughbred, Warlord came to us because he had a reputation for bucking off his riders and/or running away. Yet this powerful horse had good reasons for his behavior. He has a scar on his withers where he was ridden by a saddle so ill-fitted it drew blood, he has a spur scar on his right side, and his tongue was nearly severed by a harsh bit. For Warlord, being ridden meant pain and confusion. I can only guess at the terror and anxiety he suffered when being saddled.

Before coming to us, he had been ridden by people who gripped with their legs to stay on. Being a sensitive horse, he responded by going faster. Rather than trying to understand what was happening and correcting the problem, his former riders used a double twisted wire snaffle bit, a tight tie down and spurs to control him.

When I started schooling Warlord, he fell back into his old habits of bucking and running away. The first time I asked him to trot he took off, going faster and faster and throwing in several bucks.

Instead of grabbing the reins and forcing him to stop—which was what he had experienced in his past—I simply let him work through his fear. After about ten minutes of running around the large ring, Warlord began to slow down. I then knew he was in a place to listen and used gentle check-releases along with voice to ask him to slow to a trot. He responded very well and we had few problems in his training after that.

Today Warlord goes nicely on the bit, enjoys jumping and will take special care of a young, beginner rider. This horse has an amazing heart, is willing and clearly loves to be ridden and useful. He is eager, loves to interact when he's around people and even displays jealous behavior if we are handling another horse before riding him. He whinnies at us when we come to the barn and is ready and waiting at the gate.

Warlord is expressing healthy fourth chakra energy. Horses engaging a clear and open fourth chakra energy are fun, pleasant and exciting to ride and seem to enjoy the rides as much as their humans. The rider will often feel the horse is picking up her thoughts and responding before she even executes a signal.

When my students reach this level of energetic connection with the horse, they often make comments such as, "That was so easy!" "He just did it!" or "I hardly had to turn him at all!"

In the fourth month the rider begins to feel the energetic connections of the higher chakras. The horse now trusts the rider not to hurt, scare or confuse him, becomes comfortable and accepting of the rider's decisions and is willing to cooperate with her commands.

By the fourth month of training, the horse now has the strength and agility to carry a rider in a more connected fashion, which means the hindquarters are connected to and in balance and rhythm with the forehand. With this increased ability to balance with a rider, the horse finds it much easier to respond to the rider's wishes and will do so fluidly and efficiently. The response becomes more energetic both physically and through the chakras.

The rider can now begin to establish a *soft* contact with the horse's mouth, allowing the horse to extend his head and neck in a relaxed fashion. The horse is now capable of balancing more toward the hindquarters and engaging them while carrying a rider. To remain in balance with the horse, the rider also begins to ride primarily seated in the saddle rather than in the forward balance position.

Next three to six months: Contact and riding in company

FOURTH AND FIFTH CHAKRAS

GOAL – Develop a two way dialog between horse and rider.

The rider is ready to begin contact work when she is able to balance on a moving horse without using her hands or legs to hold on. It is easier for the rider to learn contact on a horse already schooled for contact work. The same is true for the green horse because it takes a rider with the ability to provide consistent contact along with give and take to help a horse learn to accept the rider's hands.

To achieve a consistent contact with good give and take, the rider must have a secure seat that allows her hands to be independent of her body and of each other.

SIGNS THE HORSE IS READY FOR CONTACT:

- The horse is well stabilized at the walk, trot, canter and halt.

- The horse is naturally carrying his head higher—above the shoulder line.
- The horse is going quietly both inside and outside the ring and over low jumps.
- The horse feels more agile with the rider and feels balanced and rhythmical.

30. The rider is ready to begin contact work when she is able to balance without using her hands or legs to hold on.

To prepare a horse for contact work, the rider begins by sitting down for transitions. The rider asks for a walk from a trot and sits down in the saddle in rhythm with the horse as he slows his speed. The rider should also be asking for different speeds within each gait and can use the rhythm and balance, such as increasing or slowing the speed of her posting in the trot, to signal for these changes. Such exercises will increase the horse's longitudinal agility.

Rather than using the forward balance position to transition from the walk to the trot, the rider now sits as she asks the horse to trot and rises into her posting as the horse takes his first few trot steps. The rider can now begin sitting for transitions to the canter through the trot and from the canter to a walk through the trot. All transitions should be soft and responsive, but not abrupt.

The rider should also begin to sit the trot and the canter when on the flat. It is extremely important that she is able to ride with balance, spring and rhythm so as not to abuse the horse's back. Sitting the trot and canter should only be done with a very soft contact as the horse does not yet have the muscles to carry the rider seated at the trot and canter while on the bit.

> **While sitting transitions and gaits, the rider must be able to ride with balance, spring and rhythm so as not to abuse the horse's back.**

If the horse is continuing to respond quietly with a relaxed back and neck, the rider can now begin some more intricate lateral agility exercises such as the position left and right, using the inside leg, also called holding leg, to push the horse deeper into corners. The rider can also add simple leg yields and other basic lateral exercises. These exercises should be done with one rein on contact (the indirect rein) and the other rein (the inactive rein) semi-loose or long. The inactive rein should be used occasionally to support the active rein to prevent the horse from simply turning.

For example, working the horse in a position left, the rider uses the inside holding leg and the outside urging leg described in Chapter 11. The left rein is the active rein and should be used as an indirect rein in front of the withers, also described in Chapter 11. The right rein is the inactive rein and should be kept loose except to correct the horse's speed or return the horse to the railing if he does not respond to the leg.

For position right, the aids are the same, used from the opposite side. When executed correctly, the horse will flex his jaw just enough for the rider to see the bulge of his inside eye while walking or trotting in a straight line. The purpose of this exercise is to begin teaching the horse to softly flex his jaw to the rider's hand.

31. Position left (shown here) and right are excellent lateral agility exercises to use when introducing the horse to contact.

These exercises can be physically and mentally stressful to the horse and should be used in small amounts at this level. A good beginning is performing the exercises once or twice within a session and repeating them once or twice more during the week.

Once the horse is responding well to the transitions and the increased lateral agility exercises on a loose or semi-loose rein, he is ready to begin soft contact. This contact work is begun at the walk. The rider should use her legs to ask the horse to increase his impulsion. Only after the horse increases his impulse forward should the rider take up the slack in the reins until she has a soft feel of the horse's mouth. It is best to start the contact on a large circle since the horse is slightly bent and giving to the rider's leg.

The horse may move his head around, try to stretch his head and neck forward or even come behind the bit. It is extremely important that the rider keep her hands steady and continue asking for quiet, rhythmical, forward impulsion with the leg. The rider must not punish the horse or try to correct his head position beyond keeping the hands in place and the leg asking for impulse forward.

If the rider keeps her hands quiet and continues asking the horse to come forward, he will find where his head is most comfortable. This will allow for a soft contact and not overly stress the horse.

As the horse accepts the contact and softens in the jaw, the rider should also soften her hands slightly as a reward. This softening can be as little as a relaxing of the muscles in the fingers or a slight forward give of the elbows, usually as little as half an inch.

> **Attempting to correct the horse's head position with the hands will only unbalance and upset the horse.**

At this stage, contact should be only in small doses such as a few strides, and only in the ring. The rider should ask for contact only once or twice during the first few sessions and only in one or two sessions during the week.

As the horse becomes more comfortable, the rider can increase the time on contact to a circuit or two around the ring. She gradually increases the frequency of contact work as the horse gains comfort and strength.

Once the horse achieves contact at the walk, the rider can begin using it at the trot and gradually let it flow into transitions and longitudinal and lateral agility exercises.

Transitions and turns should be done with the rider using her legs to move the horse forward into a soft "give and take" of the hands rather than the more primitive check release with loose reins. Turns should incorporate the urging leg and the holding leg in cooperation with the rider's hands.

> **It is extremely important to continue loose rein work along with the work on contact. This keeps the chakras clear and open and the horse relaxed.**

Even advanced riders wishing for a high level of energetic connection with their horse, should ride thirty to fifty percent or more of their time on loose, or at least semi-loose reins (often called a long rein by Dressage riders). This keeps the horse's chakras clear and open and the horse relaxed and trusting its rider.

Riding in company outside the ring:

During this stage of training, the rider can exercise the horse in company outside the ring at all gaits on loose reins. Riding in company outside the ring reinforces the energy in the second and fourth chakras, creating a strong relationship between the horse and rider. Hunter exercises for riding in a group make an excellent training tool that helps keep the horse stabilized and connected to his rider in spite of the company. If the rider has been successful with her schooling up to this point, the horse will listen to her more than to the other horses in the group because the horse feels safe and is connected with the rider. *Common Sense Horsemanship* and *Schooling and Riding the Sport Horse* are good sources for more information on hunter exercises.

> **It is important while riding in company that the rider be conscious of her mount and continue his schooling during the ride.**

As much as possible, such rides should be done on loose reins. The rider should require the horse to stand quietly and wait for her to signal him to move forward or to continue past the group until she tells him to stop. The horse should also be willing to leave the other horses when the rider asks.

While in company, a horse unwilling to listen to his rider or leave the other horses still has some stuck energy in his first and second chakras. Clearing and retraining these areas using exercises described in phase one will address this problem.

> **A horse unwilling to leave other horses still has energy stuck in his first and second chakras.**

Next six months to two years: Riding on the bit and flexions

FIFTH AND SIXTH CHAKRAS

GOAL – Enhance the communication between horse and rider. Develop the horse's agility and mind. Increase the quality of performance.

The horse is now ready for more advanced work, which requires a higher quality of communication and performance. In this stage the horse can begin allowing the energy to flow from the third chakra through to the fifth (this flow of energy is often called impulsion). As the impulsion flows forward the rider uses the bit to softly ask the horse to flex his jaw. The rider then redirects the energy in whichever way she desires by opening or closing space with her hands.

For example the rider creates space for the horse to turn by giving slightly with the outside hand and using her legs to ask the horse to move the energy forward into the space. This creates a flexion in the horse's jaw, and the appearance of roundness in the horse's body, rather than the rider pulling on the rein to turn the horse.

The horse is now willingly cooperating with the rider's guidance or wishes and is listening and understanding her more subtle communications. The horse is also ready for higher jumping and faster speeds such as galloping outside the ring.

SIGNS THE HORSE IS READY TO BE ON THE BIT AND READY FOR HIGHER JUMPING AND SPEED:

- The horse accepts contact work quietly and responds softly and precisely to all exercises.
- The horse is making soft transitions with the rider using give and take with the hands.
- The horse is jumping combinations and courses at least 2 ½ feet high inside and outside a ring.
- The horse canters quietly outside the ring over uneven terrain on loose reins and remains at even speeds.
- The horse listens to his rider when in company and will remain stabilized at any place (following or leading) within a group of other horses.

The rider may now begin using flexions in her turns and transitions. At this level, transitions should be precise and quick while remaining soft. Exercises for this work can include trotting from a halt or halting from a trot, work at the shoulder-in, counter-canter and change of leads with a short interruption. Other exercises at this level include:

Serpentines at the canter
Half passes
Half turns on the haunches
Turns on the forehand
Smaller circles and turns at the trot and canter
Backing
Galloping
Hold hard at the gallop
Jumping over three feet

The rider can take the horse outside the ring on trails and expose him to some unusual circumstances such as bridges, creeks and obstacles along the trail. It is recommended the horse go in company with quiet, experienced, older horses or alone with his rider. If the rider goes out alone, she should be sure to follow such safety precautions as taking a cell phone and/or letting someone know where she is and when to expect her back.

The horse should be worked on these types of exercises for a few months before moving on to semi-collection and riding fast in groups and over fences. This way, the horse builds the strength, agility and strong emotional stability required for performing in his seventh chakra.

As with humans, seventh chakra energy is high voltage. This is where we take a strong and serious look at ourselves (or in the case of the horse, his training) to see if we are ready for the connection to the Sacred.

After one year or more: Energetic connections and collection

SEVENTH CHAKRA

GOAL – Continuous connection with the horse's Sacred energy. Increase the horse's strength, his agility and the quality of communication and performance of the horse and rider.

Connecting with the horse in the seventh chakra is about creating and directing a constant flow of energy from the horse's hindquarters through the rider's hands and back through the horse again. Many riders describe this feeling as a huge ball of energy just in front of them, located around the horse's shoulders and chest.

The rider now begins asking the horse for semi-collection, higher jumping and/or speed. The horse is ready for jumping combinations and gymnastics over three feet, jumping at speed and traveling at speed over uneven terrain. It is important for the rider to continue a program of gradually strengthening and conditioning the horse for these types of riding.

SIGNS THE HORSE IS READY FOR SEMI-COLLECTION, FULL COLLECTION, JUMPING HIGHER, JUMPING AT SPEED AND TRAVELING AT SPEED IN GROUPS:

- The horse easily accepts being ridden on the bit while remaining calm and cooperative.
- The horse is able to perform on the bit for several minutes without showing mental, physical or emotional fatigue or stress.
- The horse can be ridden on loose reins and soft contact over uneven terrain for two to four hours without undue fatigue or physical, mental or emotional stress.
- The horse can be ridden quietly in groups and remains cooperative with his rider.

- The horse remains calm and responsive to the rider when ridden outside the ring in slightly unusual circumstances such as found on typical trails.

> It is easy for riders to believe that collection is the ultimate goal of riding and misunderstand that collection is one of *several tools used in training.*

If the rider wishes to pursue much riding in full collection, I recommend she study a good text on collection and work with a high-level, well-qualified Dressage trainer. She can also use several of the lateral and longitudinal agility exercises listed for work in the fifth and sixth months of training, of course eliminating the exercises that include speed, jumping or uneven terrain.

It is easy for riders to accept the popular belief that collection is the ultimate goal of riding and to lose track of the fact that collection is one of *several tools used in training.* The purpose of collection is to build strength, agility, communication and a high quality of performance for riding. In fact Littauer often states that because full collection uses high, non-efficient movement, it is not only unnecessary in training a cross-country horse, it has no place in that type of riding.

The same can be said for a Western horse. High quality collection is not necessary for a Western horse to perform well on trails, in speed events, working cattle or simple rein patterns. If the Western rider wishes to pursue higher quality reining work, she and her horse will need some training in semi-collection and flexions. She will also need to build the horse's strength and agility.

> **NOTE:** *Collection is an often misunderstood and misused word in the horse world. Many riders believe collection is gained by holding the reins tightly enough to get a "headset" from the horse. Others think collection is about putting the horse in a "frame."*
>
> *As with most riding, collection is about balance. The horse shifts his weight from the forehand toward the hindquarters and the forehand is lightened. The key word here is* lightened.
>
> *True collection is so soft and subtle the rider will feel as if she is holding gossamer threads in the tips of her fingers. The horse lowers his hindquarters, flexes in his jaw and raises his head so that his poll is his highest point and his face is perpendicular to the ground. The horse is* extremely *soft and light on the reins.*
>
> *If the rider is pulling the reins or strongly holding the horse, then he is not in true collection. If the horse's poll is lower than the crest of his neck and the face is behind the vertical, then the horse is behind, rather than accepting the bit. Such a horse's back will be stiff and hollowed out rather than soft and round.*

While it can take years for the horse to become strong enough to carry the rider for any length of time in full collection, riders can achieve a continuous connection through the horse's seventh chakra once he has the ability to perform in semi-collection.

When in semi-collection the rider will be able to feel a clear connection both to the horse and to the Sacred through the horse's seventh chakra. Such connection enhances the horse's performance and the communication between the horse and rider to the extent they seem to read each other's minds. This communication appears soft and effortless because the horse and rider are no longer communicating merely through basic signals, but also energetically.

Though it is a very good practice to train an all-around horse who can perform in Dressage, jumping, reining or at speed, it is important to note that full collection, jumping or speed is not necessary and perhaps not suited for all types of riding. A rider wishing to specialize in a particular style of riding can develop a Sacred connection with her horse using one or possibly two of these three extremes without having to fully utilize all three.

For example, as Littauer stated, using full collection is not necessary for a horse intended to perform in the hunt field or hunter/jumper shows. (Hunter/jumper shows were originally designed to judge a horse's suitability for fox hunting and for jumping, but with today's "hunt seat" style of riding—toes turned in, gripping in the knees and using the reins to balance—most of these riders rarely ride outside a ring, much less in the hunt field.)

It is also not necessary for a horse intended for high-level Dressage, Western riding or Saddle Seat to be schooled in high jumping or speed. Western horses can reach a seventh chakra connection through speed events and reining patterns or when working cattle. Though many do not realize it, properly trained Western horses actually achieve moments of collection during many of the gymnastics they perform.

Of course in Saddle Seat riding, used for gaited horses, the true goal—though rarely achieved in today's show ring—is a high quality of collection and performance.

To achieve a satisfactory connection with her horse, it is not necessary for a rider to be able to ride at full collection, high jumping, high level reining or at speed. However, using the Sacred Connections Horsemanship system gives a rider the opportunity to advance to these levels and develop a connection that is deeper and more consistent.

> Once the horse and rider have connected through the seventh chakra, they will remain connected even on loose reins or on the ground.

Once the horse and rider have achieved this deep connection, they will remain connected *even on loose reins or from the ground*. Through this connection the rider can signal the horse when on loose reins by simply shifting her seat or balance in the saddle. The horse remains light and responsive to the rider's body weight, seat bones, hands and legs.

When the seventh chakra is clear and the rider and horse connect through it to the Sacred, the connection remains as long as the rider does not violate the horse's trust. This can easily be seen even when the rider is not in the saddle as the horse will often watch his rider from across a field.

Horses who have been consistently ridden with such a deep connection will usually trust their rider in unusual situations. This was well illustrated when my Thoroughbred walked quietly through tunnels, over bridges and through city traffic during our nine-hundred-mile ride from South Carolina to Ground Zero in New York City.

> The seventh chakra connection is an ongoing relationship that remains as long as the rider does not violate the horse's trust.

As seen through this program outline, in order to build and keep the horse's trust and cooperation, it is essential to have a clear and consistent form of communication he can understand. Such a communication system works with the horse's natural reactions and employs kindness and fairness to be energetically effective. Chapter 10 outlines a form of communication the rider can use to work with the horse energetically.

Chapter 10
Communication Becomes Two-way

THERE IS AN OLD SAYING THAT IF A HORSEMAN (OR woman) is very, very fortunate, he or she may be blessed with one great horse in a lifetime. I have been fortunate to have three: Count Of War; his mother, Swaps' Fair Countes; and as I was growing up, my mother's horse, Me And My Shadow. I look forward to having more.

I have no words to describe the bonds I shared with these horses. This special connection that resides in the higher chakras is truly a rare and fragile gift. In fact, I was in my early twenties before I began to realize most riders never come close to the type of relationship I had with my horses.

As a young person, I had trouble understanding why my friends wouldn't accompany me as I galloped bareback down hills and over big jumps with nothing more than a halter and lead. At the time I did not realize I had learned a unique and rare system of communicating with my horses, which few riders have the privilege of experiencing.

It was years before I understood most riders dream of being able to connect that deeply with their horse. More often than not, they end up frustrated and forever chasing that elusive dream as they go round and round a ring, trying to keep their heels down.

Unfortunately we can see the dissolution of such desires everywhere in the horse world. A trip to a local show is often a good venue in which to witness such frustration and dissolution. Numerous riders yank on the reins while the horse is rushing his gaits with his head up and back hollowed out. Many horses strain against a double-twisted wire snaffle, or a curb bit, and a tight tie down while the riders' hands saw on the reins in a desperate attempt to slow their horses down or to "put their horse in a proper frame."

NOTE: *It is easy to mistake a horse who has an artificial headset and is behind the bit as being soft and responsive. This headset is often achieved by using abusive means employing gadgets that cause the horse to hold his head in place while being ridden.*

This type of treatment is often seen in Western horses with curb bits. Though the rider does not appear to use the reins much, an educated eye can see the horse is behind the bit, and the back and neck are actually stiff. The horse's hindquarters are tucked in tightly and not engaged. The horse may be moving with speed but not with impulsion. The horse is merely holding his head in position and moving his legs rather than engaging the muscles in the back and hindquarters. Their riders often give frequent small jerks on the reins to achieve this "headset." Susan E. Harris's Horse Gaits, Balance and Movement, *pages 153 through 155, contains more information regarding artificial head setting.*

Sadly, this type of behavior is prevalent in today's show rings and is fairly easy to spot in the local hunter/jumper shows. The Saddle Seat and Western shows are also a common source for such problems. Severe bits, tight reins, horses with their heads high and pulling with their backs hollowed out or horses over-flexed with a tense neck, back and hindquarters are all too common.

I sometimes wonder if these riders occasionally recall the reasons they began riding. Do they ever question what keeping their heels down and forcing their horse into a frame has to do with galloping across green fields with the sun on their backs and the wind in their hair? Do they ever think about how their horse feels and if he is happy?

What we see at these shows are all-too-common cases of horses that do not understand their rider's signals, have been rushed into a frame or certain look, or are otherwise incapable of responding correctly to the rider's signals.

In Chapter 4 we discussed how asking the horse to perform beyond his physical ability will quickly lose his trust. This same loss of trust happens when the rider uses signals the horse does not understand. In today's commercially driven horse industry, many riders feel pressured to ride "correctly" with their horse "collected" or at least "on the bit." This results in riders asking green horses to perform in the same manner as a seasoned, well-trained horse.

Not only does a green horse lack the physical ability to respond to more advanced signals, he is not mentally capable of understanding the subtleties of advanced communication. Starting a green horse with clear, simple signals allows the horse many small successes early in the training process. This builds the horse's self-confidence (third chakra) and allows him to trust the rider (fourth chakra). With the confidence that he can understand and please the rider, the horse will begin to "listen" more closely and work to understand and respond (fifth and sixth chakras) to the subtleties of more advanced signals.

Another very common problem that violates the quality of communication between horse and rider is an inexperienced rider attempting to use advanced communication techniques before she is ready. As we saw with the loose rein experiment in Chapter 1, a rider who is not perfectly balanced without using her hands, is not yet ready to ride a horse on contact, much less on the bit or collected. Riders who attempt to ride at levels beyond their ability will inevitably give unconscious signals and confuse the horse.

Good communication between horse and rider creates a foundation of trust, thus opening the door to the higher chakras and establishing a two-way bond. It is only through this two-way communication that the energy is able to flow freely through the chakras and make the Sacred connection.

If the rider follows a communication system based on the chakras, she can balance her signals to match the energy patterns of the horse. This assures she will be using signals to which the horse is physically, mentally and emotionally capable of responding.

In addition to developing the mental ability to understand his rider's signals, the horse must also develop the emotional maturity to focus on a task for increasingly longer periods of time. Though proper signals produce a natural reaction in the horse, it is the subtleties that refine the results and define the required period of concentration for a task.

An excellent example of such subtleties can be found in the difference between a leading rein used to turn a horse in phase one (first through third chakras) and an indirect rein of opposition behind the withers (in which the action of one rein is angled toward the horse's opposite hip) used to move the horse sideways.

A leading rein requires little of the horse except to stretch out his neck and follow the direction of his nose. An indirect rein of opposition behind the withers requires the horse to engage his hindquarters, come through his back, lift his poll, become soft in the jaw and shift his weight toward his outside hind leg. He must then flex his legs and cross them without getting tangled up, all the while carrying the rider who is sitting directly over his core muscles.

The difference between the two types of reins is only a few degrees in the angle of the hand, yet the two reins ask for a completely different response from the horse. Requiring a green horse, who does not have enough emotional maturity, to handle these subtleties can easily confuse and upset the horse.

Just as the rider builds the horse's physical agility and mental capacity with repetition of simple, basic signals, she can use simple, basic signals to create healthy emotional responses in the horse. A horse begins by naturally responding to all outside stimuli either out of survival instincts (first and second chakras) or out of self-confidence and trust (third and fourth chakras). Once the horse has moved into his higher chakras, he can engage his mind (sixth chakra) and learn a deeper understanding and response to more subtle signals.

There are four phases of communication, which correlate to the horse's lower and higher chakra patterns. By assessing the horse's current mental and emotional status, the rider can determine which energy patterns, and therefore which chakras, the horse is engaging.

By correlating the phases of communication to the horse's chakras, the rider can determine the development of the horse and adjust her training program to fit the horse's needs. The rider can then bring the horse up through the phases and corresponding chakras to engage the sixth chakra: the energy of the mind and thought. The next step is a two-way connection between the horse and rider to the Sacred found in the seventh chakra energy.

> By using a systematic method of communication based on the chakras, the rider can be certain she is using signals the horse can understand.

Communication with a horse can be divided into four phases reflecting the lower and higher chakra energies.

FOUR PHASES OF COMMUNICATION

1. Non-interfering – first, second and third chakras
2. Trusting – fourth chakra
3. Cooperating – fifth and sixth chakras
4. Enlightened – seventh chakra

32. During the Non-interfering Phase of training, the horse and rider communicate through the first three chakras.

*33. In the Trusting Phase of training, the horse connects with
the rider through the fourth chakra—the heart chakra.*

*34. In the Cooperating Phase of training the horse flexes
in the jaw and willingly cooperates with the rider,
engaging the energies of the fifth and sixth chakras.*

35. In the Enlightened Phase of training the horse and rider reach a deep energetic connection through the seventh chakra.

It is not necessary for all riders to achieve all four phases to obtain a Sacred connection through their horse's seventh chakra. As discussed in Chapter 7, once the rider and horse have developed trust through the fourth chakra (phase two), the rider has access to the energy of the higher chakras. She can then, at times, establish a Sacred two-way connection, even when employing the non-interfering seat, which is used primarily in the first phase of communication. This connection can be very satisfying for many riders and works quite nicely for trail riding and beginning-level showing.

Those riders who wish to increase the frequency and longevity of those moments of Sacred connection will need to continue with the other phases of training. The third phase engages the fifth chakra through which the horse willingly cooperates with the rider. This creates a more agile horse, capable of responding to softer, more precise communication.

Most riders find this agility and deeper communication better suited for higher level showing, hunting, working cattle and many Western riding activities such as reining and speed events.

Riding in the fourth phase of communication establishes a continuous state of Sacred connection between horse and rider. The rider influences the horse's movement in order to achieve a high quality of performance. This phase of riding includes higher jumping, riding at speed, semi- and full collection and higher levels of showing or reining patterns.

It is important to note that truly riding through the seventh chakra is fairly rare in today's fast-paced, commercially influenced equine industry. It takes time to develop a horse with the physical, mental and emotional strength to properly engage this energy for extended periods.

> **Riding through the seventh chakra for extended periods of time is fairly rare in today's fast-paced, commercially influenced equine industry.**

Unfortunately the majority of riders and trainers today are unwilling, or perhaps financially or otherwise unable, to put in the time or expense to develop such a horse. Many rely on people not understanding the difference and will use shortcuts to gain a "look" similar to this level of riding.

To the uneducated eye, the horse appears to be collected, but is instead simply over-flexed at the poll with a hollow back. Another example is the horse jumping high, but rather than being relaxed, he is rushing with his back hollowed out, legs over-tucked and his head up. Riders who take such shortcuts will often use a standing martingale (a tie-down) to prevent the horse's head from coming up.

*36. Improperly fitted tie downs, also known as
standing martingales, prevent the horse
from using his head and neck to balance.*

In the Western arena, one can also spot the stressed horses by the tight tie-downs or over-flexed head set. Even though his head is down while the horse is performing intricate reining patterns, it is the tie-down and/or a strong bit that forces the horse's head to stay in place. The horse's back is hollow, and he is usually behind the bit. Riders or trainers who do not use tie-downs may inflict other severe training methods to force the horse's head down and nose in, usually behind the bit.

It seems the widespread use of martingales became more popular in the late 1970s and 1980s. Before that I rarely saw them used, and if I did see them, they were adjusted correctly and much more loosely than is the fashion today.

This overuse of tie-downs may be evidence that many riders are not reaching a true connection with their horses.

If the horse and rider were working through trust and communication, the horse would flex his jaw and lower his head through cooperation rather than force.

> **If the rider uses trust and communication, the horse will flex his jaw and lower his head through cooperation rather than force.**

The dedicated rider who desires to reach a true connection with her horse will of course, be willing to invest the time and effort involved in developing the horse's physical, mental and emotional ability to reach this level of communication. Such development requires a logical progression of advancement from one phase to the next.

Tracking the horse's ability to advance from one phase to the next is made simple through the identification of goals, the expected performance and the aids associated with each of the four phases of communication.

Non-interfering phase – first, second and third chakras

GOAL: Clearing and opening the horse's chakras—especially the first three. Both horse and rider learn balance, relaxation and simple communication. The rider becomes the leader through the second chakra, thereby developing authority over the horse.

AIDS: The rider uses loose reins, voice commands, check release, tapping or kicking leg and stabilization. Aids are simple and clear, but primitive. The rider learns to understand the horse's basic reactions.

PERFORMANCE: Gaits are simple and primitive with the horse's head and neck extended and usually carried below the withers. The rider uses a non-interfering seat, mostly in forward balance position. The horse is balanced primarily on the forehand.

Trusting phase – fourth chakra

GOAL: Connection and trust through the fourth chakra. The rider is secure and confident with clear signals. The horse is calm, relaxed, happy and confident.

AIDS: The rider maintains a light contact with the horse's mouth. The rider uses some give-and-take with the hands and a squeezing leg. The rider's hands and legs occasionally work together and occasionally work with the horse's efforts.

PERFORMANCE: The horse is calm and relaxed at all gaits with more balance, connection and impulsion than in the non-interfering phase. Though more balanced, the horse is still on the forehand. The horse's head and neck are somewhat extended, but raised to a level above the withers.

Communication is softer and more precise and the horse is more agile and responsive. The horse's forehand and hindquarters have more connection through the fourth chakra.

The rider's seat is still non-interfering, but more seated in the saddle, using the forward balance position for uneven terrain and jumping. The rider and horse are connected through the fourth chakra.

Cooperative phase – fifth and sixth chakra

GOAL: The horse's willing cooperation with the rider through the fifth chakra, resulting in increased agility and a higher quality of connection and performance. Communication between horse and rider becomes two-way with much give-and-take. The horse thinks about the rider's signals and gives an appropriate response.

AIDS: The horse is on the bit and flexes in the jaw. The rider uses aids similar to those of the trusting phase, but with more subtlety and in cooperation with the horse.

PERFORMANCE: Soft, precise control and higher quality of performance result through cooperation of horse and rider. The horse is balanced more toward the hindquarters, understands more subtle signals and is capable of responding properly to those signals, enabling higher jumping and controlled speed.

The rider is seated at most times with her seat working in full cooperation with the horse. The horse and rider consistently connect through the fourth, fifth and sixth chakras.

Enlightened phase – seventh chakra

GOAL: Highest quality of performance and precision in all gaits, also while high jumping and at speed. The horse is agile, responsive and capable of performing calmly in high stress situations and at physically and mentally taxing levels. Rider and horse achieve a continuous connection through the seventh chakra.

AIDS: The rider uses semi- and full collection on the flat. Her hands and legs are in full cooperation with the horse's movement when in full collection or at speed, over difficult terrain and over high jumps.

PERFORMANCE: The horse exhibits a high quality of performance, agility and strength in all aspects of riding, which can include riding over difficult terrain, semi- and full collection, high jumping and speed. He has the ability to respond quickly and precisely in high stress situations, creating a continuous connection to the Sacred.

> **Used properly, aids will produce a natural, stress-free reaction in the horse.**

Though all phases require the horse and rider to be in balance, unity, rhythm and communication, each phase necessitates different degrees of subtlety and quality.

For example, phase one uses the same leg position as used in phase four to urge the horse forward, but the application of the leg is different. A tapping or kicking leg is excellent to teach a green horse to respond to the leg, but if used on a highly trained horse performing in phase four, the horse would most likely over react or possibly bolt.

Another example is the check release–a very simple and primitive precursor to the half halt–yet a green rider is not capable of producing the subtleties of hand and leg coordination required of a proper half halt.

If used properly, the aids will correspond with the phase of training in which the horse and rider are riding and produce a natural, stress-free reaction in the horse.

In order to produce a stress-free, easily understood reaction in the horse, the rider can observe the horse's normal responses to outside stimuli. All horses will naturally reproduce these responses when they react to the rider's signals.

For example, if the rider taps the horse with her heel in the urging leg position described in Chapter 11, the horse will move forward to get away from the tapping. If the rider pulls out with a rein, the horse's head will follow the pull and his body will follow his head. Therefore the horse turns.

This may sound simple, yet an inexperienced rider can easily confuse the intricacies involved in communicating with a horse. This can happen when the rider gets a rein too long or too short or changes the angle of the rein, resulting in frustration for both horse and rider. If the horse is upset or frustrated, it is impossible for him to trust the rider. If the rider punishes the horse for not responding as desired when she uses an incorrect signal, the horse feels betrayed. Of course this betrayal also violates the trust energy in the fourth chakra.

> Unjustifiable punishment will betray the
> trust energy in the horse's fourth chakra.

I believe communication between horse and rider is as misunderstood as collection. Story books and movies present an unrealistic picture of "horse whispering" achieving fairy tale results in a few days or even hours.

Common problems with communication between horse and rider today often happen when training methods attempt signals that are too advanced for the horse. This often occurs when the method does not allow sufficient time for the horse's mind, body and spirit to develop enough to understand and properly respond to the signals.

The horse also experiences confusion or frustration when the training method uses signals that do not transfer well from the ground to the saddle.

Good communication is not about achieving some esoteric level of mysticism. It is reached by:

- Understanding how the horse perceives outside stimuli.
- Knowing how the rider affects the horse mentally, physically and emotionally.
- Following a logical progression of development of the horse's understanding and physical abilities.
- Always preserving the horse's trust through non-interference, fairness and consistency.

By defining, understanding and practicing clear, simple signals, the rider can build the trust (fourth chakra) necessary for the horse to willingly cooperate with her guidance (fifth chakra). The horse then becomes capable of understanding communication on a higher level (sixth chakra) and can increase the quality of performance and connection with the rider. These signals come in the form of both natural and artificial aids, discussed in Chapter 11.

Chapter 11
Tools for Natural Communication that Works

I REMEMBER A DAY WHEN KATIE WAS RIDING WARLORD over a low jump. Katie was still learning to jump and was not expecting him to canter after the jump. Since he is a Thoroughbred and nearly 17 hands, Warlord has a BIG canter. Katie, who was used to 14.3 hand Quarter Horses, was caught off guard.

Though her mount was going quietly, Katie became frightened and grabbed one rein and then the other in an attempt to slow the horse down. Warlord easily reverted to his training and started performing flying-canter-lead changes. He was simply doing as his rider asked, though she was unaware she was signaling the horse.

I stepped to the center of the ring, spoke to Warlord, and he quickly slowed to a walk.

Katie took a few deep breaths and thought about what happened. "Poor boy. I'm so sorry I confused you!" she said, stroking his mane. Warlord dropped his head, breathed a big sigh, and the two continued jumping successfully.

This misunderstanding between Warlord and Katie is a good example of how easily signals can be misinterpreted. Katie was attempting to use a primitive signal to slow the horse, yet she unknowingly used a more subtle version of the signal, which resulted in a higher level of response.

Since the aids are basically the same for each level of communication, it is the level of primitive versus educated that determines the subtlety involved. Through an understanding of the application and effect of the natural aids, riders can match the complexity of the aid to their own and the horses' level of training and ability.

For example, a beginner rider or an experienced rider on a green horse will use a tapping or kicking leg to signal the horse. The more experienced rider on a trained horse will use a squeezing leg in cooperation with the hands and the horse's movements. In each case, the horse increases his impulsion forward.

While both leg signals are used in the same vicinity, it is the subtleness of the squeezing leg, combined with the hands, that results in a higher quality of forward movement.

The aides can be divided into the following categories:

NATURAL AIDS	ARTIFICIAL AIDS
Voice	Whips
Stabilization	Spurs
Body Weight	Bits
Legs	Martingales
Hands	Side Reins
	Draw Reins
	Sticks
	Weighted Reins
	Other Equipment and gadgets

Artificial aids should *only* be used 1) as correction if the horse does not respond to a natural aid and 2) to increase the level of communication between a schooled horse and rider.

Examples: Using the tap of a whip if the horse does not respond to the leg or using a double bridle for a high level of performance in full collection.

Unfortunately some riders and trainers misinterpret the purpose of artificial aids and believe they can be used as control devices or to shortcut quality training methods. A common example of such misuse can be seen in the numerous types of bits, along with a great deal of misinformation regarding their function and purpose.

> **Bits are communication tools not brakes.**

While some riders believe all bits are cruel and refuse to use them at all, others, not understanding how they function, can easily mistake a severe bit for a mild one because the former has a joint. I strongly urge all riders to study a good text on bits and become familiar with the way they function and affect the horse.

The most important thing for a rider to understand is that *bits are communication tools* not *brakes*. All horses, when properly trained, can be ridden in a light snaffle or even a halter. If not, then it is up to the rider to examine her skills. Many riders can be successful using a halter in phases one or even two. It is only for the higher communication engaged in phases three and four that a bit becomes a *useful*, but *not necessary*, tool. Proper increase in the leverage of the bit is used *only* to improve the quality of communication, *not* the level of control.

I believe this is a good time to address some of the more recent fads regarding bitless bridles, "liberty training" and other efforts attempting to discover a kinder, gentler way of interacting with horses. While most of those working in these areas have good intentions, I question whether they are truly making a difference in the horses' world.

For example, if we examine the recent fad of bitless bridles with an educated eye, we can discover, that similar to a hackamore, a bitless bridle, especially in uneducated hands, will actually put more pressure on the horse than a soft bit used by an educated rider on a trained horse. In the hands of an uneducated rider, a bitless bridle can also inflict more pressure on the horse than a soft bit used with loose reins.

So many riders, not understanding how bits, spurs, whips and other such artificial aids are designed to be used, misinterpret their function and level of severity. With that in mind, it is important to emphasize the following:

- Bits are communication tools, not brakes.
- Control comes through communication, education, agility and cooperation, not through leverage.
- All horses, when properly trained, can be ridden in a light snaffle or even a halter. If not, then it is up to the rider to examine her skills.
- Increasing the leverage of the bit should be done only to improve the level of communication, not the level of control.
- Just as with bits, spurs are used to increase communication, not to make the horse go.
- A mild blunt spur is usually sufficient. If the rider requires more, then she should work on her communication skills and the training and abilities of the horse.

- The rowels on Western spurs, used correctly, slide the spurs along the horse's sides, not inflicting damage as is usually imagined and are not intended to make the horse go faster.
- Spurs should only be used by educated riders on well-schooled horses.
- Used correctly, whips are not intended to beat the horse, but to back up a rider's insufficient leg signal, to increase the horse's forward energy or to increase the horse's focus.

Spurs can be viewed much like bits because they are used *to increase the level of communication,* not to make the horse go faster. Used properly, a blunt spur can finesse the communication of the rider's leg for a higher level of performance.

Spurs should be used *only* by riders with a secure seat and an independent, educated leg. They should be used *only* on *schooled horses* capable of fully cooperating with the rider's hands and legs working together.

There are applications in which side reins, martingales and other artificial aids can be judiciously used to aid in training. However, they are more often used as shortcuts or as a "quick fix" to poor riding or training. I will always advocate first identifying the problem and attempting to re-school the horse or rider.

> **The rider should always use the softest aid first.**

By understanding the application of the natural aids, the rider can more easily identify how to match their use with the horse's level of training.

Since the rider is attempting to build trust and encourage the horse to "listen" and willingly cooperate with the aids, she should always choose the softest aid first. The rider can compare this use of soft aids to a person speaking quietly first, then increasing the volume of his or her voice until heard. It is the whispered sounds we listen for and the loud annoying sounds we tune out.

Horses are the same. If they are given soft, subtle signals, they will begin looking for the signals and become more responsive and focused. The harsher or louder the signal, the more the horse will either try to get away or tune it out. Since the voice does not physically impact the horse, it is considered the softest aid. The aids are listed below with the gentlest first.

Voice

The rider uses voice primarily when riding in the non-interfering phase on loose reins to clear and open the chakras. Once the rider moves into the trusting, cooperating and influencing phases of the higher chakras, the rider no longer uses voice, except upon occasion in schooling.

VOICE CAN BE USED IN FOUR WAYS:

1. Go-faster voice – strong, sharp and commanding – to ask the horse to increase his speed
2. Go-slower voice – slow, soothing, but clear and with gentler command – to ask the horse to slow down or stop
3. Praising voice – enthusiastic, happy, but not shrill – to praise the horse for cooperating
4. Correcting voice – sharp, commanding – to stop the horse and get his attention – *generally only used from the ground*

The horse can learn to recognize several simple words. The rider can try using "walk," "trot," "canter," "hoa," "slow," "good boy" or "good girl," "settle" and "quit." The one-or-two-syllable words are excellent when strongly enunciated for a go-faster voice and can be dragged out somewhat for a go-slower voice.

If the rider uses "hoa" instead of "whoa," the horse does not so readily confuse the "w" sound in walk. Hoa should be used only to ask the horse to stop. She can use "slow," enunciating the "s," to slow the horse down within the gait. Use of a command followed by "out," such as "walk out," is excellent for increasing the speed within the gait.

The praising voice for "good boy" or "good girl," along with a food reward such as a handful of oats or a piece of carrot, is an excellent way for the horse to associate the voice and words with reward for good behavior. Chapter 13 contains more information on the use of voice and food for reward.

> Horses' ears can become dull to commands in a similar fashion as their sides and mouths can become dull to legs and reins.

If the rider uses too many words, horses' ears can become dull to commands in a similar fashion as happens when their sides and mouths become dull to legs and reins, respectively. I must often remind riders that the horse does not understand "Come on now, let's go" or "Let's go, Trigger" or other versions of chatter many riders employ. All commands should be kept clear and simple.

Body Weight

The next aid in order of least severe is body weight. If used correctly, body weight can gently signal a horse to increase or decrease his rhythm or speed, turn or even stop. Used incorrectly, such as in the case of an unbalanced rider or bouncing seat, body weight can abuse or hurt the horse.

The rider can cause the horse to increase his speed by leaning forward. If the rider sits deeply into the saddle, she can cause the horse to slow down or even stop. Leaning to one side or dropping the weight to a seat bone or into a heel can be a signal for a horse to turn or move sideways.

If the rider speeds up the rhythm of her posting, the horse will respond with a faster trot or lengthening of his stride. Slowing down and softening the posting can cause the horse to slow his rhythm or speed.

Once the rider learns to control her balance, and thus her body weight, she can use it in all phases of riding and work within the different chakras. When the rider is forward and off the horse's back, she allows the horse to clear and open his first, second and third chakras. If the rider sits in the saddle and adds a light contact with the horse's mouth, she can ask the horse to connect the third and fifth chakras through the fourth. By shifting her weight to the deepest part of the saddle, the rider asks the horse to shift his weight toward the hindquarters and to lift and engage his seventh chakra.

Legs

Legs are usually listed before hands in order of softest aids because after phase one, all of the horse's movement should come from the energy created by the rider's legs rather than a pull on the reins. When the rider uses her legs, she creates the energy that flows through the horse's chakras, which is then directed by the rider's hands. Used correctly, the legs actually do more of the turning and stopping of the horse than the hands.

A horse who does not respond to the leg is said to have dull sides. Dull sides are usually a matter of energy stuck in the second (relationships) and/or fourth (heart) chakras. This is often a result of heavy or abusive legs such as when a rider grips with her knees or calves to stay on.

It is possible to "re-awaken" a horse with dull sides by using a proper **tapping or kicking leg** such as used in the non-interfering phase. The rider increases the amount of pressure if the horse fails to respond to lighter use.

Just as with the other aids, the legs are used differently depending on the level of ability of the horse or rider. Simple leg aids, such as tapping or kicking, are used primarily when clearing the first three chakras using the non-interfering phase of riding. When engaging the higher chakras and riding in the trusting, cooperating or influencing phases, the rider uses a squeezing leg in cooperation with her hands and the horse's movements.

A tapping or kicking leg helps the rider learn:

1. How much action it takes to get a response from the horse
2. Improved control of her legs

A tapping or kicking leg helps the horse:

1. To more clearly understand and "hear" the rider's signals
2. Develop softer, more responsive sides as he "listens" for the rider's signals

There are three basic leg aid positions:

1. **The urging leg:** The rider's leg is used slightly behind the girth to urge the horse forward.
2. **The holding or bending leg:** The rider's leg is used on the girth to move the horse onto his outside shoulder and outside hind leg in a turn.
3. **The displacing leg:** The rider's leg is used well behind the girth to move the hindquarters, such as in the turn on the forehand.

*37. The urging leg is used slightly behind the
girth to urge the horse forward.*

A squeezing leg used in cooperation with the hands causes the horse to perform with his jaw relaxed and his hindquarters engaged. If the rider uses her legs to create forward energy in a turn, the horse will engage his hindquarters, be more balanced and better carry himself and the rider through the turn.

Unfortunately, in an effort to ride in a manner they perceive as "correct" or in a misguided effort to advance a horse's training too quickly, many riders attempt to use advanced leg signals before the horse is ready. A green horse, or a horse dealing with first or second chakra issues, simply either cannot understand the subtlety of, or cannot properly respond to a squeezing leg.

38. *The bending or holding leg is used on the girth to move the horse onto his outside shoulder and hind leg in a turn.*

39. *The displacing leg is used well behind the girth to move the horse's hindquarters.*

Rein aids

As with all aids used in Sacred Connections Horsemanship—with the exception of the neck rein, which must be taught to the horse—the rein aids produce a natural reaction. Even if the rider uses an educated rein aid on a green horse, he will attempt a correct response, though it may be stiff and primitive. In order for the horse to respond correctly to the educated rein aids, the horse must have the muscles and agility to respond.

In the early stages of training using Sacred Connections Horsemanship (phase one), both the horse and rider begin with simple, primitive rein aids. This includes using loose reins, which naturally produce primitive signals. By using loose reins, the inexperienced rider can avoid accidentally hurting the horse if she loses her balance and unintentionally jerks a rein.

Loose reins allow the green horse to fully stretch his head and neck, which clears and opens his chakras. As the horse learns he will not be jerked in the mouth, he develops trust in the rider, knowing he has the full use of his head and neck for balance.

Once the horse or rider move into phase two of training, the rider picks up a soft, but definite contact with the horse's mouth. At this point the rein aids become more subtle and are supported by the rider's legs.

With the exception of the leading rein, the rein aids look the same whether they are used as primitive or more advanced signals. It is the looseness of the reins or the contact with the horse's mouth that determines the degree of subtlety.

> **Loose reins prevent the inexperienced rider from accidentally hurting the horse if she loses her balance.**

Simple Rein Aids

Simple, primitive rein aids are an easy and effective tool for clearing the chakras and are strongly recommended for use in the non-interfering phase of communication.

SIMPLE REIN AIDS INCLUDE:
- Loose or looped reins
- Semi-loose or long rein
- Check release for slowing down or stopping
- Leading or opening rein for turning

40. Loose reins allow the horse to clear and open his chakras.

LOOSE OR LOOPED REINS

To prevent the horse from feeling restricted at all, the reins must be long enough to have a loop in them. This length will allow enough room for the balancing gestures of the horse's head and neck. Otherwise the horse will feel a catch in his mouth every time he moves his head and will slow down, stop, become tense or begin to ignore the rider's hands.

Benefits Rider: The rider can learn to balance without the concern of hurting the horse's mouth or giving conflicting signals.

Benefits Horse: On the energetic level, loose reins allow a free flow of energy from the first through the fifth chakras. They are excellent in helping to open and clear the horse's fifth chakra because they allow the horse to physically open and stretch his jaw.

On the physical level, this type rein allows the horse the looseness necessary to stretch and develop muscle quality.

SEMI-LOOSE OR LONG REIN

Semi loose reins, often called "long rein" are not so long as to have a loop in them, but there is still no contact with the horse's mouth. The rider must be able to move her hands with the balancing gestures of the horse's head and neck, so as to avoid jerking the horse in the mouth. It is recommended only to be used by an experienced rider who does not need her hands to balance.

Benefits Rider: The rider can quickly regain control of a horse that is not well stabilized or is unpredictable.

Benefits Horse: On the energetic level, a semi-loose rein still allows for the free flow of energy similar to that when using loose reins. On the physical level, this type rein allows the horse the looseness necessary to stretch and develop muscle quality.

CHECK RELEASE

The rider brings her hands back far enough to feel a brief moment of tension on the reins, then moves the hands forward. Check release can be used with either one or both reins depending on the desired result.

Whereas a pull will cause the horse to respond with a corresponding pull, and will dull his mouth, a check release will break up any resistance from the horse. It will also help reclaim a dull mouth, making it soft and responsive.

Benefits Rider: Check release is a primitive precursor to a half halt and helps the rider learn the use of hands when she has not yet mastered the subtleties of give and take. Check release offers the rider basic control without confusing or hurting the horse as she learns her balance.

Benefits Horse: The release part of the check release allows the horse room to stretch from the head through to the thoracic area as he transitions to a slower gait or a halt. As the neck stretches forward, the energy flows through the jaw, clearing and opening the fifth chakra.

41. The leading or opening rein allows the horse to stretch his head, neck and back in a turn.

The rein aids and their application:

1. LEADING OR OPENING REIN – Primitive rein used in the non-interfering phase and primarily connected with the first three chakras. The rider takes one rein within twelve to eighteen inches from the bit and brings it out and *forward*. This rein is used to turn the horse while the opposite rein remains very loose.

Benefit for rider: The rider learns to separate the use of her hands from her balance and to use each hand individually.

Benefit for horse: The rein allows the horse to extend his head and neck resulting in a free flow of energy from the first through the fifth chakras. This rein does not contract the horse's muscles or slow the horse down.

2. ONE REIN OF DIRECT OPPOSITION TO THE REAR – Primitive or educated rein used primarily in the higher chakras. When on contact, on the bit or in semi- or full-collection, the direct rein is designed to *only* close space and redirect the energy flowing forward. The rider does *not* pull the rein back or outward at all. In the second, third and fourth phases, this rein is *always* used in some degree of cooperation with the rider's legs.

When on contact, on the bit or collected—trusting, cooperating and enlightened phases—at the walk or canter, the rider simply ceases to follow the balancing gestures of the horse's head and neck with this rein while the opposite hand continues to follow the horse's head movement. When at the trot, the rider simply shortens the rein, usually by increasing the bend in her fingers. The opposite hand remains soft, allowing space for the horse's jaw to flex and the horse to continue forward movement. The rider continues to use her *leg* to ask the horse to move forward.

This results in the horse's muscles on the inside of the turn contracting while the outside muscles extend, creating a curve in the horse's neck and pushing the rib cage outward. The horse's strides follow the bend of his neck through the turn. When used in the third and fourth phases for turns, the rider pushes the horse to the outside direct rein by adding an inside leg and merely taking up the slack in the outside rein. A direct rein of opposition to the rear will slow a horse down.

This rein is rarely used with loose reins in the non-interfering phase, but when employed, the rider can use it with a simple check release without the leg. In the non-interfering phase this rein is primarily used alongside the railing to slow the horse down. The opposite rein stays loose.

42. One Rein of direct opposition to the rear (shown here)
helps the horse learn to soften in the jaw and
carry himself well balanced through a turn.

Benefits for rider: With loose reins, the rider can use one hand on the rein to slow the horse's speed while the other hand remains on the horse's mane to help the rider maintain her balance. When used on contact, on the bit or collected, in cooperation with her legs, the rider does not have to pull and risk abusing the horse's mouth in order to turn.

Benefits for horse: With loose reins, the horse begins to learn to slow down by contracting his muscles and giving slightly in the jaw in preparation for contact. When riding on contact, the rein will cause the horse to carry himself well balanced through a turn. When riding on the bit, or collected, the horse will flex to the rider's hands, engaging the third and fifth chakras.

3. Two reins of direct opposition to the rear – Used to slow down or stop the horse when in the non-interfering and trusting phase. Used to contain and redirect the energy flowing forward from the horse's hindquarters when on the bit or in semi- or full-collection. As with all other reins, the rider does *not* pull the reins.

With loose reins in the non-interfering phase, the rider uses both reins simultaneously in a check release motion to slow down or stop the horse. This action is a primitive precursor to the half halt.

On contact—trusting phase—the rider either tightens the fingers or stills the hands, then gives slightly in rhythm with the horse's strides. This rein is also used to slow down or stop the horse. Again the rider *does not pull.*

When riding on the bit or collected—cooperating and enlightened phases—the rider uses varying degrees of give and take as needed to contain the energy flowing forward from the horse's hindquarters. For a slower pace, stop or back, the rider simply keeps the reins still or closes the bend in her fingers *while adding leg.* If the horse does not slow down, stop or back, the rider *adds more leg.*

Just as with the single, direct rein of opposition, the rider does *not* pull on the reins but simply holds the hands still or closes the bend in her fingers while adding leg. The horse's body will contract and the horse flexes his jaw.

Benefits for rider: A novice rider using the non-interfering or trusting phases can slow down or stop the horse without abusing his mouth. A more experienced rider using the cooperating or enlightened phases can contain and direct the horse's flow of energy through the higher chakras, thus gaining a deeper communication and higher quality of performance.

Benefits for horse: With loose reins or light contact, this rein allows the horse room to stretch his head and neck and keep his jaw soft. This enables him to more easily balance the rider through the downward transition. This allows the horse to stretch his neck and shoulders and loosen his jaw, thus clearing and opening his third and fifth chakras.

When the horse is on the bit or in semi- or full-collection, the rein causes the horse to flex in the jaw and shift his weight toward the hindquarters, engaging the third and fifth chakras. If the rider is using the rein to signal a reduction in speed or to back up, the horse will respond with his jaw relaxed and hindquarters under him.

4. INDIRECT REIN OF OPPOSITION IN FRONT OF THE WITHERS – Used to move the horse sideways or to the outside of a turn while the horse remains slightly bent toward the inside. It is typically reserved for working with the higher chakras through the cooperative and enlightened phases. It can be introduced in the trusting phase if used softly with the opposite rein kept fairly loose.

The action of one rein is angled toward the rider's opposite hip. The angling is accomplished by a slight (between one and two inches) movement of the hand toward the horse's neck. The rider's hand does *not* cross the horse's neck. This rein should always be accompanied with a holding or bending leg on the same side and an urging leg, used as needed, on the opposite side.

The rider should only begin using this rein as the horse develops the ability to connect his third and fifth chakra by engaging his back muscles in a turn. The rein is usually not introduced until the horse begins work in his fourth chakra. In the early stages of using this rein, the rider should keep the opposite rein fairly loose.

Benefits for rider: The rider can move the horse toward an object such as the railing, or around an object such as a hole, without disturbing his forward movement.

Benefits for horse: This rein helps the horse learn to engage his hindquarters and balance through turns with his back relaxed and hindquarters engaged. The rein also helps the horse strengthen the back and respond with a soft flex in the jaw.

43. An indirect rein of opposition in front of the withers shown here, is used to move a horse to the outside of a turn while he continues to flex in the direction of the turn.

5. Indirect rein of opposition behind the withers – Used mostly to combat severe resistance of a horse. When used in the higher chakras, it encourages the horse to shift much of his weight toward the hindquarters and lift the poll.

The action of one rein is angled toward the horse's opposite hip. The angling is accomplished by a slight (a few inches) movement of the hand toward the horse's withers. The rider's hand does *not* cross the horse's neck. The opposite rein maintains light contact or is kept fairly loose, depending on the application of the rein.

This rein is fairly severe and is generally reserved to combat extreme cases of resistance such as bucking, kicking or rearing.

44. The indirect rein of opposition behind the withers, shown here, is severe and should generally be reserved for dangerous misbehavior in the horse.

Benefits for rider: In extreme cases of the horse's mis-behavior (such as in bucking), the rein can be used to place the horse on his opposite hip and throw him slightly off balance, allowing the rider to regain some control. *The rein should be used very judiciously only by educated riders.*

Benefits for horse: In the hands of an educated rider, this rein can engage the horse's third through seventh chakras by asking the horse to shift much of his weight toward the hindquarters and lift the poll. This helps increase the horse's collection, strength, agility and quality of performance.

THE NECK REIN

The neck rein does not produce a natural response in the horse and therefore must be taught to the horse.

This rein is used today primarily by Western riders who need one hand free to throw a rope. No doubt the neck rein was also employed by military riders needing a free hand to hold a weapon such as a bow, sword or revolver. This rein used correctly by an educated rider on an educated horse typically engages the fourth, fifth and sixth chakras.

> **The neck rein does not result in a natural response from the horse, and is therefore, the only rein that must be learned by the horse.**

The rein is pressed along the side of the horse's upper neck and turns the horse in the opposite direction of the rein. The rein *must* be taught using an inside bending leg and an outside urging leg. It is essential to keep the rein *loose* in order to avoid pulling the horse in the wrong direction.

The neck rein itself does not actually signal the horse to turn as much as do the rider's legs. An educated horse with the physical ability to properly balance with a rider through a turn will quickly learn the neck rein by responding to the correct use of the rider's legs.

If the rider attempts to neck rein a horse before it is physically and mentally ready, the horse will be stiff and unbalanced, often with his mouth open and resisting the rider's hands. An attempt to neck rein a horse without the proper use of legs will result in the same stiffness and resistance.

Benefits for rider: The rider has the free use of one hand.

Benefits for horse: Rather than stepping through a turn, the horse actually pivots, using less space, allowing him to turn faster and react more quickly, ideal for a horse when working cattle.

45. The neck rein (shown here) is the only rein that does not produce a natural reaction and must be taught to the horse.

Before the horse is ready to properly respond to educated reins, he must trust the rider to not accidentally jerk him in the mouth or otherwise misuse the reins. Horses can feel the slightest movement of the reins, even when not on contact.

Most of my horses in phase one will respond to the mere weight of the rein changing and will turn before there is any tension placed on the rein.

Unfortunately, many riders believe their hands are soft or they are riding on loose reins simply because they do not have constant contact with the horse's mouth. Other riders are taught to ride on contact by imagining they are "holding a thousand pounds in their hands."

Regrettably, these misconceptions result in horses with dull mouths and riders who pull on the reins to drag their horses around. Both wind up frustrated and unable to communicate beyond a crude, and sometimes harsh, inflicting of orders. The horse remains in the survival energy of the first chakra, and the rider is frustrated because the horse does not lower his head, flex in the jaw and become soft.

NOTE: I would like to caution riders on the recent fads of using weighted reins and thin, jointed, shank bits. Horse's mouths are so sensitive they can feel the slightest change in the weight of a rein. Therefore it is important for the rider to be cautious of weighted reins currently used in some methods of Western riding. If the horse's mouth is not dull from severe bits or uneducated hands, he will be very sensitive to the constant pressure inflicted by weighted reins.

If the horse's mouth is dull, it will be extremely difficult to reclaim the sensitivity while using weighted reins, because there is no way to remove the constant pressure the horse will experience.

NOTE: Another current development, especially in Western riding, is the use of very thin, jointed, shank bits. As with the weighted reins, in the case of a thin, jointed, shank bit, the horse feels the slightest movements of the rider's hands. The use of either of these two devices often results in the horse overflexing at the poll in an effort to evade the constant pressure they are experiencing.

Of course it is not just the Western riding style that has experienced problems with gadgets used to short cut quality training methods. The hunter/jumper show ring is filled with riders using double twisted wire snaffles and standing martingales adjusted too tightly. In fact this has become so prevalent that many hunter/jumper riders–and even many trainers–believe all horses should be ridden with a tight standing martingale as regularly applied equipment.

For many years the world of gaited horses has been plagued with long shanked bits, built-up shoes and other gadgets used to force the horses to move artificially for the show ring.

> **The proper use of loose reins helps the horse clear and open the first through the fifth chakras.**

Whereas a highly skilled rider can softly allow the horse to relax, stretch and clear his chakras while on contact, most less experienced riders do not usually have such balance. Therefore, loose reins are an excellent tool for clearing and opening both the lower and higher chakras. With loose reins, the horse can trust the inexperienced rider to not accidentally jerk him in the mouth or otherwise misuse the reins.

The horse's mouth is much more sensitive than a rider's hands, therefore it is easy to inflict a great amount of pressure on a horse without realizing it.

An advanced rider can also use loose reins to allow the horse the room to relax and stretch. Loose reins can also prevent even the most capable of riders from being caught off guard by a green horse and accidentally violating the horse's trust.

The following is an excellent exercise to gain a true understanding of the horse's sensitivity to the reins:

NOTE: Hold the top of a bridle in one hand and place your other hand, palm up, around the bit. Have a friend hold the reins very loosely in both hands as if she were riding a horse.

Now close your eyes and ask your friend to slowly take up the slack in the reins. The instant you feel any movement in the reins, ask him or her to stop. Now open your eyes and notice how loose the reins still are.

Next, try this again but instead of having your friend take up the slack, have him or her establish a soft contact and merely tighten the fingers of one hand. Can you feel the movement?

If you consider that the mouth, even a horse's mouth, is much more sensitive than our hands, you begin to understand the amount of pressure you can inflict upon your horse. No wonder so many horses become upset and uncooperative!

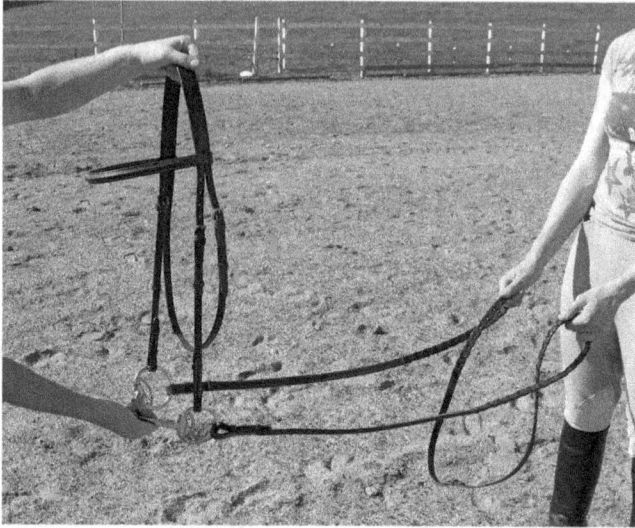

*46. As shown in the picture of this exercise, a rider can
experience the pressure inflicted by a bit by holding
it in her palm while another moves the reins.*

Balance and movement

Communication between horse and rider cannot be reasonably addressed without examining balance and movement. Body weight (the rider's balance) is not only used as an aid but will also strongly influence the horse's ability to listen. In order for the horse and rider to communicate, they must be in balance and in unity as explained in Chapter 4.

The aids and styles of communication will only be effective if the rider understands the horse's natural movement, instincts and responses. Once the rider understands the horse's reactions, she can use the natural aids to create a particular result from the horse. Chapter 12 discusses the horse's natural movement, instinctive behavior and related responses.

Chapter 12
Understanding the Horse's Natural Reactions

L ILLIAN AND I WERE WORKING ON SIMPLE TURNS ONE DAY. She had a lovely little chestnut Quarter Horse mare that was quiet, sweet and very willing; perfect for a rider to learn simple aids.

As Lillian turned the horse with a primitive leading rein, I asked her to tap the mare's opposite side with her heel. The mare engaged her hindquarters a bit and moved forward through the turn more easily.

"If you poke a horse in the side, the horse will move away from whatever is poking him," I said. "If we understand this, we can obtain a natural response from the horse by using a simple aid. If you kick a horse with the left foot, he will move away from the kick—forward and to the right."

Lillian laughed and said, "Duh, *I* would."

I seriously considered writing a book entitled *Duh Horsemanship.*

> **Horses will respond naturally to certain stimuli if the rider understands when and how to push.**

Just as Lillian learned, understanding how the horse responds to certain stimuli allows the rider to create a desired response in him. *The key is understanding when, where and how much to push.*

This understanding can be discovered by studying the four basic areas from which the horse draws his reactions: instinctive, physical, emotional and mental.

THE HORSE'S NATURAL BEHAVIOR CAN BE DIVIDED INTO FOUR MAIN CATEGORIES:

- **Instinctive** – how the horse responds naturally – first and second chakras
- **Physical** – how the horse moves and balances – first, second and third chakras
- **Emotional** – how the horse relates current events to his present feeling of safety and to former good or bad experiences – fourth chakra
- **Mental** – how the horse responds to training – fifth and sixth chakras

When the horse moves beyond instinctive, physical, emotional or mental responses into energetic response, he enters the seventh chakra. While working through seventh chakra energy, the horse no longer responds primarily to physical signals from the rider but connects directly with the rider's energy through the Sacred.

47. When the horse moves beyond instinctive,
physical, emotional or mental responses into
energetic response, he enters the seventh chakra.

By working with the horse's natural responses, the rider can help the horse understand her wishes. By understanding and working with the horse's natural responses, the rider can avoid asking the horse to perform above or outside of his ability.

Therefore the horse continues to feel safe. When the horse feels safe, he will give a positive response, thus moving his energy toward the higher chakras. A negative response based on fear will keep the horse stuck in first- and second-chakra survival energy.

The Horse's natural behavior

INSTINCTIVE – FIRST AND SECOND CHAKRAS

The horse's instinctive responses are stored in the first and second chakras. These are "move first and think later" reactions that keep the horse (a prey animal) alive in the wild.

THE HORSE'S BASIC INSTINCTS CAN BE RECOGNIZED IN SEVEN
FORMS OF BEHAVIOR:

1. HORSES ARE PREY ANIMALS – The horse is an herbivore and
therefore does not hunt or attack other animals. His major
defense is to run away. If the horse is frightened or threatened,
he will first try to run away, shy, bolt, rear, buck or use other
forms of evasion. It is important to remember that though
they are domesticated and familiar with people, a *horse's first
reaction will be to view humans as predators.*

The rider can reduce the threat a horse automatically
feels around humans by speaking softly, eliminating fast or
threatening gestures, providing food and treating the horse
fairly and gently. Another very effective method of removing
any threat perceived by the horse is to be certain the horse
is not in pain from poor riding, a poor fitting saddle or from
working when he is sore or lame.

2. HORSES ARE CREATURES OF HABIT – If the wild horse returns
each spring to the field where the grass grows early in the
season, or each winter to the protected canyon, he increases
his chances of survival.

For most horses, it takes repeating something only a couple
of times for a habit to form. This especially happens with
undesirable behavior!

A rider can use this knowledge to encourage good habits in
the horse by allowing him to repeat desired behavior. She can
also discourage undesired behavior in the horse by stopping
such behavior before it becomes a repeated habit.

3. HORSES ARE HERD BOUND – In the wild, the isolated
horse is a dead horse. Therefore he will always feel safer
with other horses.

If the rider keeps in mind the horse will usually want to be
with other horses, she can use stronger signals when leaving
the herd, or she can walk her horse quietly toward other horses

rather than allowing him to run. If the rider uses clear, decisive signals and makes safe decisions when riding, her horse will feel safe with her and respond first to her, rather than focusing on the other horses.

4. HORSES ARE IMITATORS – A horse will usually do what the horse in front of him does. If the horse in front suddenly jumps sideways, the horses behind him will usually jump sideways as well. This might save them from the pouncing panther or keep them from falling off a cliff. In the wild, the horse who reacted immediately without stopping to think was better able to stay alive.

When in the company of other horses and riders, a rider can use this instinct by observing the other horses and being prepared for her horse to follow them. It is a good practice for the rider to train the horse to wait for *her* signal rather than always allowing him to follow the other horses. This allows her to stay in control. The rider can also use this instinct to school a green horse by allowing him to follow a more experienced horse through a ditch or over a jump.

5. HORSES ARE DRIVEN BY THE NEED FOR FOOD – Without the supplement of grain, horses must eat large quantities of grass to stay alive. It is amazing what horses will do for food.

Contrary to all his instincts, a horse will walk into a dark stall or even a small horse trailer if offered a bite of his favorite grain. The rider can use this instinct to enhance training by rewarding desired behavior with a bite of food.

6. HORSES HAVE GOOD MEMORIES – A horse has an excellent memory. In the wild the horse stays alive who remembers where the water is during the drought or where the salt lick is.

The horse who spooked at a certain spot on the trail will most likely spook in that spot the next time. The horse ridden when he is sore or not cooled out and rubbed down properly will remember that riding hurts and will be reluctant to be caught the next time.

7. HORSES HAVE A STRONG HOMING INSTINCT – Horses will always try to return to their home, remembering home is where they will find food, shelter and safety.

The old saying "Never run your horse to the barn" is acknowledging this instinct. Good horsemen understand the horse will go faster in the direction of home and can adjust their riding and training to accommodate this instinct. An experienced show rider will often ask her horse for more impulsion when the course is heading away from the ring gate than when heading toward it.

> **Unless the horse is taught differently, when he encounters outside stimuli, he will drop into the instinctive reactions of the first or second chakras.**

Without proper training, when the horse encounters outside stimuli, he will drop into the instinctive energy of the first or second chakras. The horse will then respond with one of these seven basic forms of behavior. If the rider truly understands how the horse will react, she can use this knowledge to create a desired response in the horse.

As the rider works with the horse's natural responses to obtain desired, rather than instinctive behavior, she begins to develop the horse's self-confidence, trust and eventually his cooperation. This engages the higher chakras (third, fourth and fifth) and he relies less on instinctive reactions such as running away.

PHYSICAL – FIRST SECOND AND THIRD CHAKRAS

The horse's physical responses can be divided into two categories: **movement** and **balance**, which work together.

Obviously the horse must be somewhat balanced in order to move without stumbling or falling down.

However, once a rider mounts, the horse must relearn to balance with the added weight and movement of the rider. The more balanced the horse, the more easily he can carry himself and the rider while obtaining a higher quality of movement.

Balance is achieved through strength and agility, which directly connect with the self-confidence of the third chakra, located under the saddle. This area from the top of the horse's back through the belly behind the girth area contains the bones, muscles and ligaments the horse uses to carry a rider. The common saying of having the "guts" to do something directly correlates to the area of the third chakra, the stomach/solar plexus region.

If the rider allows the horse natural movement and balance, she supports not only the horse's physical ability to carry her, but also strengthens the horse's self-confidence and trust. This increases the horse's ability to develop a higher quality of movement.

Therefore the physical aspect of the horse's natural responses moves through the third and fourth chakras. A rider who understands the horse's movement can support the development of the horse's balance and agility through these chakras.

A CLEAR UNDERSTANDING OF BALANCE AND MOVEMENT ALLOWS THE RIDER TO:

- Give the horse the freedom to move naturally.
- Create exercises that develop the horse's natural balance and agility.
- Redirect that balance and agility into a desired performance.

> The rider's balance directly affects the relationship
> between herself and the horse's feeling of safety.

MOVEMENT:

Littauer described movement as "the constant loss and regaining of balance forward." In other words, the horse simply pushes his weight forward until he loses his balance and places a leg out in front to catch it again. If the horse continues to repeat this process, his legs are constantly moving, thus creating movement forward.

Just as we use our arms to balance, the horse uses his head and neck to shift his weight forward and backward. When the horse prepares to move, he must first shift his weight off the leg he is going to move. The horse accomplishes this by lifting his head up and back to shift his weight to the hindquarters, thus freeing the front legs. When his head is out and down, the horse's weight is more on the forehand, freeing the hind legs.

These balancing gestures are used primarily at the walk, canter, gallop and when jumping. Gaits such as the trot or pace are more balanced and use the thrusting of the legs for movement more than the shifting of weight.

Though the horse can move without free use of his head and neck, it is difficult and will stress his joints and muscles.

Horses ridden by someone who balances themselves with the reins or uses a tight tie down can be compared to a person trying to run and jump over uneven terrain with a moving weight on her back and her arms tied to her sides. She would experience soreness in her back and legs and would have great difficulty balancing and even risk an injury or a fall.

By studying the movement of the
horse's legs at the various gaits, we can
better understand how he balances.

A rider who understands the horse's movement at the various gaits is more equipped to accurately signal a horse as well as follow the balancing movements of the head and neck. Such a rider can also quickly discern if the horse is unsound, stiff, unbalanced or otherwise off in his movement.

Below is a description of the basic natural gaits. For descriptions of gaited movement such as the pace or rack, consult Susan E. Harris, *Horse Gaits, Balance and Movement.*

WALK: A FOUR-BEAT GAIT WITH LATERAL MOVEMENT

- Right hind
- Right front
- Left hind
- Left front

TROT: A TWO-BEAT GAIT WITH DIAGONAL PAIRS

- Right hind and left front
- Left hind and right front

CANTER: A THREE-BEAT GAIT WITH ONE DIAGONAL PAIR

Canter-LEFT LEAD:

- Right hind
- Left hind and right front
- Left front

Canter-RIGHT LEAD:

- Left hind
- Right hind and left front
- Right front

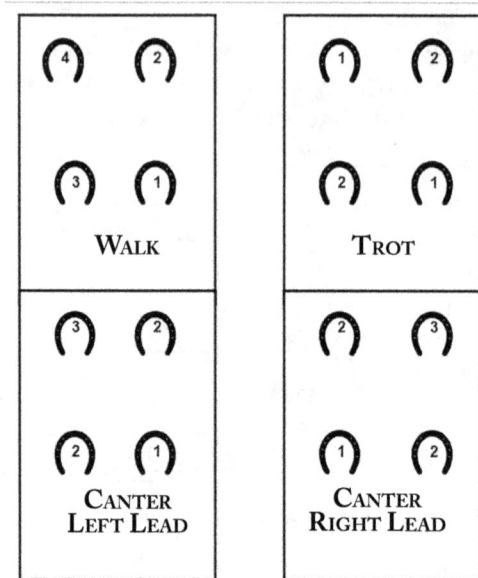

47. Knowing how the horse moves his feet at the walk, trot and canter allows a rider to more accurately signal the horse.

The trot is more balanced than the canter or the walk because it uses an upthrusting of the legs more than redistribution of weight for the forward movement. This results in little or no balancing gestures of the head and neck. Because the trot is well balanced, forward and rhythmical, it is ideal for basic schooling such as in low jumping.

As the horse becomes stronger and more agile, he can use his muscles more to affect his balance. As he becomes more balanced with the rider, he can easily handle more intricate movements.

BALANCE:

A dictionary definition of balance is: "a state of equilibrium or equipoise; equal distribution of weight." It is through distributing her weight equally with the horse's weight that the rider remains in balance with the horse.

So often I hear of instructors telling their students to sit back on the horse, or lean back when they ask the horse to stop, or even lean back when going downhill to "counterbalance" the horse's weight. I find myself wondering why the rider would ever wish to "counter" the horse's weight because this puts the rider completely out of balance and therefore forever prevents her from becoming "one with her horse."

48. A rider out of balance with the horse, as demonstrated by this rider whose balance is too far back, will make the horse feel unsafe and prevent unity between the two.

The rider's balance directly affects the relationship between herself and the horse's feeling of safety (second chakra). A rider who is out of balance with the horse will, at the very least, impede his quality of movement. At worst, she can cause the horse confusion and pain or put them both at risk for a fall.

If the horse is feeling the pain of a rider's weight hitting his back or hands grabbing his mouth for balance, he does not feel safe. This unsafe feeling escalates when he is asked to travel at speed, over uneven terrain or over jumps without the ability to use his head and neck to balance.

However, if the horse learns he can trust the rider, he will open his second, third and fourth chakras and allow the energy of trust to flow between the two of them. This creates not only a physical unity and balance between them, but also creates an energetic balance.

An understanding of how the horse naturally balances will help the rider understand how to match her balance with the horse.

49. When standing still, three-fifth's of the horse's weight is on his forehand, as shown here.

THE THREE TYPES OF A HORSE'S BALANCE ARE:

1. Static – The horse's balance while standing still. Three-fifths of the horse's weight is on the forehand.
2. Dynamic – The horse's balance while in motion. The horse's weight shifts from the forehand through to the hindquarters and back to forehand again, depending on the horse's speed and the terrain.
3. Central – The horse's balance when collected. The horse's weight shifts from the forehand toward the hindquarters and the forehand is lightened. This is a natural reaction the horse uses when he is frightened or startled.

50. When in Dynamic Balance, the horse's weight shifts from the forehand to the hindquarters and back.

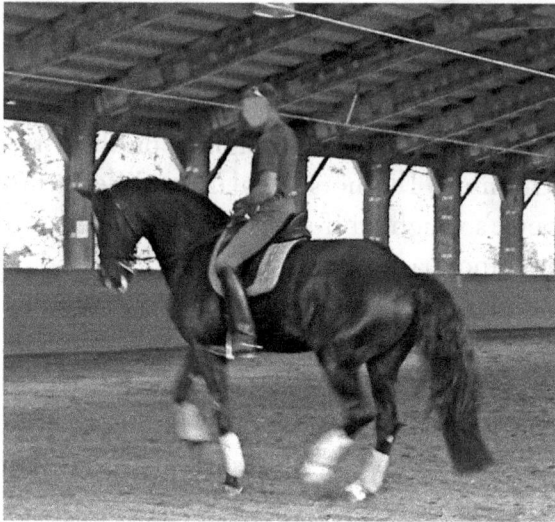

*51. When in Central Balance, the horse's weight
shifts from the forehand to the hindquarters
and the forehand becomes lighter.*

Once the rider understands the three types of balance, she can determine which one the horse is currently using and place herself in the saddle to best match his balance. For example: When the horse is traveling at speed, he will be using dynamic balance and will have more of his weight on the forehand. A good illustration of this is a racehorse in full gallop.

If the horse shifts from speed to intricate gaits with a high quality of movement such as in Dressage or Western reining, the rider will want to sit deeper and slightly farther back in the saddle, allowing the horse to lighten his forehand.

A horse being ridden on a trail or cross country primarily employs dynamic balance. The horse will shift his balance from the forehand to the hindquarters and back in order to accommodate the various speeds and types of terrain he is traveling. The rider must have a dynamic seat capable of shifting her weight to stay in balance with the horse.

I think it is important here to address the misconception many riders have that all horses should be ridden "on the bit" or "collected" at all times. In the natural state the horse employs central balance only when threatened or when moving suddenly. Central balance (collection) naturally stimulates the horse's adrenalin and places his body and instincts on high alert.

When a rider asks the horse to perform in the state of central balance or collection for more than a brief moment, she triggers this adrenalin reaction and creates physical, mental and emotional stress in the horse. The ability of the horse to continue this state of stress is in direct proportion to his strength, knowledge and agility. This is why Dressage tests begin as short rides and increase to a longer test as the horse moves up in levels and increases his strength. Dressage tests rarely last more than half an hour.

Asking a horse to perform on the bit or collected for a two- or four-hour trail ride is not only unrealistic, it makes traveling at speed or over uneven terrain extremely difficult. The result is rarely true collection, but usually a stiff and eventually nervous or uncooperative horse.

> **Asking a horse to perform on the bit or collected for a trail ride makes traveling at speed or over uneven terrain extremely difficult.**

A rider who has good balance will instill trust in the horse. This directly connects and opens the second (relationship with the rider) and the fourth (heart – trust) chakras. As the energy flows from the second chakra through the third and into the fourth, the horse will become more willing, more confident and more boldly responsive to the rider's signals. The horse is now capable of cooperating with the rider and responding emotionally and mentally, which is fourth and fifth chakra energy.

Emotional – fourth chakra

Many highly acclaimed horsemen will say that horses do not have emotions and are motivated primarily by where their next meal is coming from or by trying to avoid work. Yet if the rider observes horses closely, she can see evidence of several basic emotions and responses triggered by current and past events rather than immediate survival or propagating instincts.

It is most likely that horses do not feel and/or express emotions in the same way as humans; however that does not eliminate the existence of feelings. The more obvious emotions in horses are fear, frustration, irritation, jealousy, excitement, elation, stress, shock, tension, worry and contentment. More detailed observation will reveal signs of happiness, joy, sadness, despair, affection, boredom and various other reactions.

Many horsemen and women have reported seeing horses pine for a lost pasture buddy and show signs of jealousy when their owner rides another horse. Others have seen their horses play games with an almost "human" sense of humor. I personally recognized evidence of grief in Count for years after his mother passed away.

The rider must be prepared to preserve the horse's emotional well-being and development, just as she does the horse's physical and mental well-being and development. If a rider neglects to reward the horse for accomplishing a task, she can compromise the horse's trust and create confusion or frustration in him. Repeating an accomplished task over and over can compromise the horse's "heart" or willingness to continue performing and he will become "sour."

> **Once a horse has accomplished a task, the rider should reward him and move on to another task to prevent him from becoming sour or uncooperative.**

Another aspect of emotional response in the horse can originate from past events or traumas. I remember when I started jumping Warlord, he would rush the jump and run away after the jump.

Warlord was sound and physically and mentally ready to begin jumping in his training. He was asked to go over a very low cross rail with cavaletti, and I rode him very carefully in the forward balance position, so his back, sides and mouth were not being hurt. Yet he would get faster and faster.

Warlord was afraid. He remembered his past jumping career, which meant harsh bits, tie downs and abusive hands, legs and seat. He feared a repetition of past hurts.

We had to work Warlord for several weeks on a completely loose rein over very low jumps. I also lunged him over jumps so he could experience absolute freedom while jumping. It took a long time and a lot of patience, but he eventually realized he was not being hurt, gave up his fear and began trusting.

Warlord's post-traumatic response looked exactly the same as an instinctive response to a present threat such as pain or confusion. The difference was, he was not being hurt in the present. His behavior was an emotional reaction (fear) to a past event.

By correctly identifying the present emotional state of her horse, a rider can work to safeguard the horse's feelings and create positive experiences that foster positive responses.

As with humans, horse emotions lie primarily in the fourth chakra, the heart. It is here the horse engages the energy of trust that opens the upper chakras.

Once the horse trusts the rider, he is free to begin cooperating with her. This engages the energy of the fifth chakra. The horse usually engages this energy from an emotional state of trust, self-confidence, affection, friendship and/or even love. While horses instinctively will not cooperate with a predator (human), it is through the trust and affection they acquire for a good rider, along with their self-confidence, that horses give their *willing cooperation*. Otherwise riding is merely a matter of subduing the horse and forcing him (even when using subtle means) to submit to our will.

> **Without the willing cooperation of the horse, riding is merely a matter of subduing the horse and forcing him to submit to the rider's will.**

A horse who continuously experiences positive emotions will continuously engage his heart and spirit and be more willing to trust and cooperate with his rider. This moves the horse into the fifth and sixth chakras and engages the energy of the mind described in Chapter 13.

> **The goal of training is to engage the horse's mind—along with his body and spirit.**

MENTAL – FIFTH AND SIXTH CHAKRAS

The main goal, if not *the* goal of training, is to engage the horse's mind—along with his body and spirit. The engaged mind is well demonstrated when my horses walk quietly in busy traffic, stand calmly with gunfire around them or willingly walk through a tunnel or encounter other potentially frightening situations.

People are often puzzled to see this willing cooperation, even going so far as to accuse me of drugging horses or buying ones that were "special." What these observers are missing is that, through the system of Sacred Connections Horsemanship, my horses have shifted out of their lower chakras and engaged the higher chakra energies of trust, will and thought. Therefore, when faced with cannons thundering and smoke billowing or when asked to ride through a tunnel, my horses will stand quietly and calmly or put their heads down and willingly continue forward on a loose rein.

When these horses engage their minds, it is evident that they realize I do not put them in situations that will hurt them, confuse them or betray their trust. This allows them to set aside their fears and think about an appropriate response to what is around them, rather than simply reacting through survival instinct.

NOTE: *Although they appear similar, a horse exhibiting a calm thoughtful response is not the same as a horse responding while in freeze mode. A horse in freeze mode may be still or quiet, but he is numb with fear and cannot engage his mind to give an appropriate response. Such a horse can be dangerous because it is unknown when he might shift from freeze to flight or fight.*

For wild horses facing the challenges of survival everyday, the situation is just the opposite. In the wild, the horse who stops to think usually winds up dead. This instinct of "react

first and think later" resides in the first chakra and sets the
structure for the simple signals used in the non-interfering
phase of training. (If the rider pokes the horse in the side, he
moves away from the poke.)

Though domestic horses have this same instinctive
response, they have also learned that not all new or different
situations are necessarily life-threatening. Domestic horses
have been bred for thousands of years not only to serve
humans, but to understand and interpret combinations of
signals from their riders. Rather than just trying to get away
from a perceived threat or a poke in the side, domestic horses
are asked to respond correctly to combinations of much more
subtle signals.

In order to think before he reacts, the horse must be capable
of focusing his entire attention on the signals from his rider.
If the horse is struggling with issues of health, nutrition or
pain, he simply cannot move into the higher chakras and focus
his mind. Therefore, before attempting to work in the higher
chakras, it is vitally important the rider take care of the horse's
basic survival needs, such as nutrition, health and soundness,
which are discussed in Chapter 14.

Once the rider has addressed these survival basics, she can
command enough of the horse's attention to begin expanding
his thinking process. This engages the horse's higher chakras
and opens him for connection through the Sacred energy of the
seventh chakra. The next chapter outlines the communication
tools the rider can use to engage the horse's mind.

Chapter 13
Five Simple Basics for Easy Chakra Training

Hooves pounded as twenty horses and riders charged in close formation across the field. Metal sabers flashed in the bright sunlight, and I blinked my eyes to clear them of smoke. The ground shook as a cannon boomed fifty feet in front of our line.

"Company halt!" the captain's voice bellowed.

We slid to a halt. The horse next to me jumped sideways and slammed into Count's shoulder. Count heaved a big sigh as if to say "Newbies!" I reached down and stroked his silky red mane.

"Right into line!" the captain shouted. "Return—sabers!" Metal scabbards rattled as three-foot-swords clanked into their sheaths. "Draw carbines! Load!"

I dropped the reins on Count's neck and pulled my heavy rifle from the scabbard. I grabbed a paper cartridge and tore it open.

"Second Squad! By File! Forward at the gallop!"

Oh wow! My hands were full and I didn't want to drop the cartridge and spill the expensive powder.

But I needn't worry. Count knew what to do. He wheeled left behind the horse next to us and took off at a gallop in close formation. We raced to the top of the field and the sergeant called, "Right into Line!" Count wheeled right.

"Skirmish order, ten paces!"

"Post!" came the trooper's shout behind me. I counted ten paces at the gallop and Count turned back to the front.

"Halt! Aim!"

I poured the powder down the gun barrel, grabbed a cap and lifted my rifle.

"Fire! Fall back twenty paces!"

My rifle roared. Count spun around, galloped back twenty paces and wheeled to face the skirmish line again.

"Good job, men! We stopped 'em!"

I stared through the smoke to see the line of blue infantry falling back to the trees. I shoved the rifle back in its scabbard and realized my reins were still dropped on Count's neck. I reached down and patted his copper shoulder. "Good boy!"

"Hunter. I don't know how you control that horse in a snaffle bit," said the sergeant.

I glanced over to the gray-clad man on the nervous bright bay. The horse wore a long-shank curb bit and a very tight tie-down, typical of most of the horses in the ranks.

I glanced down at Count's soft snaffle bit. He had followed all the orders throughout that maneuver without me ever touching his reins.

"He knows what 'whoa' means," was all I could think to say.

Upon recalling that day years later, I'm not sure how many signals Count picked up from my legs and seat and how much he recognized of the shouted orders. Regardless, it was an exemplary example of a horse responding to good training through the engagement of his higher chakra energies. If at any time, Count had felt threatened by his rider, or otherwise did not trust me, he would have quickly bolted away from the smoke, gunfire, cannons and confusion.

> **Communication from the rider must be in a form the horse can understand.**

As demonstrated with Count, once the rider has acquired the skills to ride with an independent seat and understands how the horse interprets and responds to outside stimuli, she can begin communicating with the horse through the higher chakras. Such communication results in the type of responses my horses give me. However, this communication must take a form that makes sense to the horse and entices him to participate. Such communication has the following five basic aspects:

1. Fairness
2. Leadership
3. Clarity
4. Fun
5. Consistency

1. Fairness

There has been, and perhaps always will be, healthy debate in the horse world as to what defines fair treatment of horses. In recent years, training systems with descriptions such as "natural," "join up," "games," "submit" and other enticing buzz words have flooded the market. It can be quite challenging for the amateur or even a more experienced horseman or woman to sort through these descriptions and find a system that is not only an effective training tool, but will also help him or her become energetically connected with the horse.

Perhaps a good approach is to listen to the words used and observe the immediate behavior of the horses, along with the long-term, rather than short-term, results of the method. Words such as "submit" or "subdue" are not generally used in developing the energetic cooperation of the higher chakras. Terms such as "natural horsemanship" and "join up" sound as if they might be more geared for a higher level of cooperation. However, systems using these techniques generally work exclusively in the energy of the first and second chakras.

> **Riders should look beyond the words used to market a system of training and observe the long-term results.**

Observing the horse's responses to the training can help the rider determine if the training system will employ the fairness and consistency necessary to develop the trust that allows access to the horse's higher chakras. Systems that are focused on fast, early results cause many experienced horsemen and women to question the long-term effects of a horse saddled and ridden in the first thirty-minute session. In fact, well-known "horse whisperer" Monte Roberts said, "It takes two years to break and train a horse."

A system of clear, fair, consistent consequences for desired and undesired behavior will make sense to the horse, allow him to trust the rider and produce the desired results. Such a system must include not only clear corrections, but clear rewards that are understood by the horse. For more information on reward and correction, see pages 213 thru 218.

To clarify what you are seeing in a training technique, try asking the following questions:

- *Is the horse relaxed with head down and neck stretched throughout all early training sessions?*
- *Are the horse's muscles round and relaxed?*
- *Does the horse appear eager for attention and training even after several sessions?*
- *When being handled, does the horse stand quietly observing healthy boundaries?*
- *Is the horse's breathing calm, rhythmical and relaxed?*
- *Is the horse as calm and quiet in the fifth and tenth session as the first?*
- *Does the training method take into consideration the horse's physical, mental and emotional abilities before asking him to perform?*
- *Are you able to obtain a higher chakra connection with the horse from the saddle as well as on the ground?*

In Contrast:

- *Is the horse's head up, back stiff, legs splayed out and hindquarters tight or shaking?*
- *Does the horse appear to turn "at bay" ready to fight the predator?*
- *Does the system promise fast turnaround or force the horse into a frame during the early stages of training?*
- *Are the horse's muscles tight and angular?*
- *Is the horse over bitted and/or over-flexed or is he wearing a tie down?*

The story of a student who had a young, unbroken mule named "Jenny" illustrates how horses (and especially mules) react to fair, consistent treatment.

Dorothy sent the mule out for training and said the mule came back pushy and uncooperative. She felt the trainer's techniques were not fair since they required the mule to submit to all his demands whether Jenny understood them or not.

"Even when Jenny did what he asked, she was confused because there was no clear reward," Dorothy observed. "He also asked her to do things she didn't have the muscles for. I don't think that was fair."

Dorothy explained that, even more than horses, mules will not put up with unfair treatment.

"The mule trainer pushed Jenny around, always getting in her space," said Dorothy. "Jenny didn't understand what he was doing and didn't like it."

Dorothy began to employ the consistency, clarity, fun, fairness and leadership of Sacred Connections Horsemanship. After only a couple of weeks, Dorothy started telling stories about how great Jenny was responding.

"She understands what I want her to do," Dorothy said. "She really likes it."

After two months of this fair and justifiable treatment, the mule was following Dorothy around like a big dog and willingly cooperating with the slightest command.

2. LEADERSHIP

Another way for a horse to feel safe is for the rider to become a strong and clear leader. An example of the horse taking over as leader is eating grass while the rider wants to go for a ride. In such a situation, many riders commonly pull on the reins trying to regain control.

Such a scenario often begins with an inexperienced rider simply not being clear as to where she wants the horse to go. Therefore, the horse decides to take care of himself.

As with most animals, horses use a pecking order to determine the strongest and smartest of them suitable to be the leader. The herd instinctively knows the best leader will take care of himself, and therefore the rest of the herd along with him.

Domestic horses transfer this desire for a strong leader to their human handlers. From the horse's point of view, someone has to lead in order for him to stay safe and well fed. If the rider does not lead, then the horse will.

However, this search for a strong leader goes far beyond the discovery of who can boss the others. The rider must make clear, sensible decisions about what she wants the horse to do, where she wants the horse to go and at what speeds. This requires the rider to think ahead and plan turns, halts, transitions and other maneuvers.

The horse interprets this decision-making ability as the rider being aware of potential threats and planning the means of survival. The horse will then accept the rider as leader and cooperate with her commands. Confusion generated by unclear, inconsistent or unfair demands makes the horse feel the rider will not be able to provide for, or protect him. His natural reaction will be to try and take care of himself.

> **It is vital we communicate in a clear and consistent manner *that makes sense to the horse.***

3. Clarity

Just as there are many opinions about what is fair treatment of a horse, there are also many theories as to what horses can interpret from humans. Since horses cannot understand human conversation beyond a few basic sounds, it is vital for riders to communicate in a manner *that makes sense to the horse.*

A good example of confusion in horses can be seen by a recently popularized method of a person on the ground asking a horse to back up. In this method the handler stands in front of the horse (where the horse cannot see her) and shakes the lead rope. The horse raises his head, attempting to see what is in his blind spot, which stiffens and hollows out his back.

If the horse decides to back away from what he cannot see, he is forced to use incorrect muscles because his head is up and back hollowed out. Another challenge with this method is that the rider simply cannot use it when mounted.

However, if the rider stands by the horse's shoulder and pushes on the point of his shoulder while gently tugging on the lead rope and saying "back," the horse will soften in the jaw, lower his head and use the correct muscles in his back and hindquarters to step backward. If the handler adds an obvious reward, the horse will soon understand this signal for backing and will easily learn to respond to the similar signal employed by a mounted rider using her legs, hands and voice together.

Being very clear about distinguishing between desired and undesired behavior is just as important as clear signals. As with a child, using fair and reasonable correction balanced with obvious reward is an excellent way to identify desired or undesired behavior for the horse.

By observing how horses in a field correct their young or defend their own space from each other, we can see that fair and reasonable correction is not cruel or abusive.

For example, horses use their teeth and hooves very strongly—to the point of drawing blood or breaking bones. In comparison, a slap of the rider's hand or the tap of a heel is relatively mild. Therefore, just as horses use fair discipline and correction amongst themselves, the rider can use it to create safe, desired behavior in the horse.

A fair form of correction and reward employs a consistent set of consequences for the horse's actions. In Sacred Connections Horsemanship, the horse always receives either a reward for desired behavior or a correction for undesirable behavior. Defining justifiable and effective forms of correction and reward helps the rider employ a fair form of discipline that makes sense to the horse and helps him feel safe.

REWARD is a very effective means of influencing the horse's behavior. Food, soft words and kind touches will allow the horse to perceive the human as a safe zone in which his survival needs are met simply by cooperating with the desires of the human. This creates a willing attitude in the horse.

In the early stages of training, a horse must receive abundant, clear and obvious rewards for his good behavior. Types of rewards can be as much as a bucket of food or as little as the release of a checking rein.

Though many people think it teaches a horse to bite, I personally use treats fed from the hand in much of my training. I have never had a horse learn to bite, because I balance this reward with correction for biting. It is also very important to *not* aggravate the horse by handling or "playing" with his mouth.

REWARD MUST BE:

ABUNDANT – The horse should experience a great deal of reward in early stages of training.

IMMEDIATE – The reward should be offered within three to five seconds.

CONSISTENT – Each request from the rider should *always* be followed by either the appropriate reward or correction.

SOME EXAMPLES OF REWARD:
- Offering food or treats
- Releasing pressure, such as releasing a check of the reins when asking the horse to stop
- Stroking the horse – a soft stroke instead of a pat
- Using voice in a happy, upbeat way, such as "Good boy!" – not too loud or shrill
- Ending work – ending the work session on a good note before the horse becomes bored or sour

> **In the early stages of training, reward should be lavish.**

Recently popular systems of training use a cessation of pressure solely as reward. This means the rider or handler continues asking the horse to run around a pen or back and forth at the end of a rope, reverse direction, move sideways, or other types of movement, until the horse unknowingly performs or eventually figures out the desired behavior. If the horse stumbles upon or discovers what is wanted, the rider or handler then stops asking him for that particular movement. She does not acknowledge the horse's success in any other manner such as a treat, a pat or by saying "good boy."

As a sole reward, cessation of a signal is effective in higher levels of riding where the horse is engaging his mind enough to think about the subtleties involved in a two-way communication with the rider. At those levels the horse feels safe enough to focus his attention on advanced signals such as a give in the rein or a softening of a leg.

Unfortunately, using a system of cessation exclusively for reward before the horse is able to access his sixth chakra energy will confuse him and cause him to remain in the lower chakras. A green horse relates to pressure as a form of threat to survival. Therefore he will simply continue trying to get away until he either 1) stumbles onto whatever he perceives as the least threatening or 2) simply stops trying to get away and shifts to freeze mode. Either way, he will continue to feel threatened.

This method risks the horse becoming overworked, soured or highly stressed. Because the horse cannot easily recognize an obvious reward directly resulting from the desired behavior, the rider must require him to continue repeating the desired behavior several times until he can relate the particular movement to what is being asked.

We can compare this "cessation of pressure for reward" to the horse using bucking and rearing in an effort to communicate to us that the way we are riding is hurting or confusing him. For example, the horse's actions of bucking, rearing or running away could be caused by an ill-fitting saddle, a sore back or being asked to perform beyond his mental or physical ability.

Many riders misinterpret these signs from the horse and accuse the horse of being stupid, stubborn, ill tempered, or uncooperative. Until the rider stumbles upon the actual reason for the horse's behavior, the horse is forced to repeat the behavior each time in the desperate hope the rider will figure out what he is trying to convey.

Regarding the use of cessation of pressure for reward, Ann Fratcher, D.V.M. said, "How is the horse going to like someone who is always putting pressure on him and the only relief is the release of pressure? This will make the horse always want to get away from you."

> **If the horse receives an immediate reward that makes him feel safe, he will willingly try to reproduce whatever behavior led to the reward.**

A much more direct system of training, consisting of simple signals and rewards based on the horse's natural reactions, allows the horse to quickly respond without the stress of trying to discover the rider's requirements. If the horse receives an immediate and obvious reward that makes him feel safe, he will 1) more easily connect it with the desired behavior and 2) willingly attempt to reproduce whatever behavior led to it.

A system comprised only of reward can also confuse the horse and become dangerous. If the handler offers treats by hand and never corrects the horse for nibbling, the nibbling can quickly escalate into biting as the horse asks for another treat. Yet if the handler corrects the horse when he first begins to nibble, the horse quickly learns he has crossed a boundary and consequently learns to respect the handler's space.

As with a human child, when the rules are clear and consistent, the horse will feel safe and consequently observe healthy boundaries.

> **Using cessation as the sole method of reward will usually confuse or sour a green horse.**

Correction

Just as horses within a herd enforce rules and healthy boundaries, humans can, and should, correct their horses in order to help them understand the rules and feel safe. By setting healthy boundaries with her horse, the rider lets him know she is in charge and *is looking out for his welfare as well.*

Healthy boundaries also give the horse consistent guidelines for behavior he can count on. Just as with a child in a household where the rules are unclear, nothing will make a horse crazier than unclear or inconsistent rules. If it is wrong on Monday, it must be wrong on Tuesday through Sunday as well.

If we observe horses in a herd, we see they use bites, kicks and threatening gestures to correct other members of the herd. These corrections are always in proportion to the offense and rarely last more than a brief moment. These corrections are fair and justifiable within the healthy boundaries of the herd.

Humans can also use correction as a *fair and justifiable* means of setting healthy boundaries. If the correction is *always justified* and *always fits* the misbehavior, it will never be too excessive or administered out of anger. A small playful nip by the horse warrants a soft slap rather than a whipping. A harsh bite, buck or kick will need a sharper, stronger correction such as a swat or two with the whip. A soft check of the reins or a tapping leg is appropriate for a horse not responding to the voice, and a check of a lead shank is appropriate for a horse who is pushy on the ground.

Correction must also be in the *vicinity* of the crime. For a kick, the rider should use the whip on the horse's hindquarters, rather than his neck. She should gently slap the side of the horse's nose if he tries to bite. This helps the horse associate the correction with the crime.

CORRECTION MUST:

FIT THE CRIME

BE IMMEDIATE

BE CONSISTENT

BE WITHOUT ANGER OR EMOTION

BE FAIR AND JUSTIFIABLE

BE VERY CLEAR

BE IN THE VICINITY OF THE CRIME

SOME EXAMPLES OF CORRECTION:

- A check with the reins – used to slow down or stop the horse who does not listen to voice
- A swat with the flat of the hand on the side of the horse's muzzle – used for a horse nibbling or for small bites
- Turning the horse in a small circle along with three short quick swats with a crop or short bat – used for major offenses such as kicking or bucking
- A check/release with a lead shank across the horse's nose – used when the horse oversteps boundaries such as walking too close to the person leading him, walking too fast or not standing
- A tap or kick with the heels – used when the horse does not move forward in response to a proper voice command

4. FUN

It is the rider's job to entice the horse into willing cooperation with her ideas of riding. After all, horses were not born with humans on their backs, and it is not usually their idea to be ridden; at least not in the beginning.

Therefore, riding should not be fun for the rider only but for the horse as well. Unfortunately, while riders have dreamlike visions of galloping through fields and over jumps, the horse's experience is often just the opposite. All too frequently, horses feel the pull of the unbalanced rider grabbing the reins, the slap of her seat in the saddle or the crushing grip of her legs while trying to stay on the horse.

If the rider can ride in a way that does not hurt the horse, either intentionally or unintentionally, the horse can begin to enjoy their rides together. I remember Countes always wanted to explore strange trails and her son, Count, would always put in a few playful bucks when galloping through a grassy field. And who can deny the competitive drive and heart of a Thoroughbred who sticks his nose out to win a photo finish?

5. CONSISTENCY

Consistency is a very important factor in building a horse's trust, mental and emotional health and healthy chakra energies. Just as with a human child learning family and societal behavior guidelines, clear, consistent boundaries help the horse become successful in his relationship with his rider. Nothing can make a child—or a horse—crazier than inconsistent rules. Therefore it is the rider's (or handler's) job to clearly communicate to the horse desired behavior guidelines and be certain these are the same every time.

A common example of using inconsistent rules is when the rider allows her horse to push past her through a gate or stall door, then gets angry or disciplines him when he knocks her down or steps on her foot.

In such a scenario, because the discipline is not consistent, the horse simply doesn't understand or relate the anger and/or discipline to any particular behavior of his. All he knows is he can never predict when he will be hit, jerked or yelled at. Consequently, the horse lives in a constant state of anxiety, even fear, of being hurt.

Clear, consistent communication will also prevent horses from becoming anxious when they do not understand what their riders are signaling them to do. When horses do not properly respond to their signals, most riders tend to increase pressure through use of strong pulls on the reins, harder kicks or harsher equipment. Consequently their horses learn to anticipate this increase of pressure and will react with greater anxiety, becoming more difficult to control.

By setting clear, consistent guidelines through obvious forms of communication, riders not only gain trust, but create environments in which horses can be successful. This develops horses with strong third and fourth chakra energies (self-confidence and trust).

Another way to support horses' mental, emotional and energetic health is to be consistent in not interfering with their natural movement. A horse frightened of being pulled off balance, getting hit in the back or jerked in the mouth simply will not trust his rider—or be able to distinguish such treatment from intentional discipline.

As Lendon Gray said, developing trust in the horse requires the rider not to interfere with the horse's natural way of going. The rider must consistently prove to the horse that she will not interfere with his natural movement before he willingly relinquishes his ability to balance and decide where he is safe. Unless a rider is somewhat accomplished, riding without interfering requires the use of loose reins.

So often in my riding and teaching career when I have suggested a rider use loose reins, she looks at me as if I have lost my mind. Most riders believe if they let go of the reins, the horse will run away.

However, the very effective tool of stabilization will give the rider the consistency of pace she needs from the horse to be able to ride without constantly having to slow the horse down with the reins or speed him up by using her legs.

Stabilization

Stabilization is a basic foundation for Sacred Connections Horsemanship because it works with the horse's mind and engages the higher chakras early in the horse's training. Through stabilization the rider can control the horse without the use of pain, force or punishment. Therefore stabilization reduces the level of abuse and is essential to establishing trust.

Littauer defines stabilization as, ". . . the horse maintains an even speed at all gaits, whether on loose reins or contact, regardless of the terrain until the rider tells him to change." Stabilization also describes the rhythm and relaxation that make up an essential foundation in Dressage.

52. Through stabilization the rider can control the horse without the use of pain, force or punishment.

The beauty of stabilization is that the horse can be controlled without the use of force. Because the control is purely through the horse's *desire* to cooperate with the rider, the horse engages his higher chakras (fifth and sixth) and *chooses* whether he will respond to the rider's requests.

Given the opportunity, most horses respond well to stabilization training. It is easier and less work for a horse to remain in an even speed. Unless there is a physical or emotional reason, once taught stabilization, most horses will choose to remain in an even speed. Exceptions occur for reasons such as a rider's abusive seat or heavy legs, a saddle pinching the horse's shoulders or a horse with emotional or mental problems.

Stabilization also helps build the horse's self-confidence (third chakra). Being able to choose his own speed allows the horse to be in a place of self-empowerment rather than fear of the bit or leg. If the rider continues to reward the horse with kind words, strokes or even treats, the horse feels good about his accomplishment and the fact that he is successfully pleasing his rider. This continues to strengthen his third chakra area, the back.

Stabilization is first taught on the lunge line and then transferred to the saddle. The rider should use a non-interfering seat with the forward balance position and loose reins when first teaching stabilization from the saddle. This assures the rider of not interfering with the horse's natural movement and allows the horse to settle comfortably into a natural rhythm.

Stabilization also allows for the free flow of energy through the horse's chakras by removing all restraints in his back, sides, neck and jaw. As the horse relaxes and stretches his head, neck and back, the energy begins to travel up the spine, clearing and opening the chakras.

> Stabilization allows the horse to *choose*
> whether he will cooperate with the rider.

Cruelty and Abuse

I believe any text about equine communication should include a frank discussion about cruelty and abuse and how these are perceived *by the horse*. It is very important to understand that the horse cannot differentiate between a tug on the reins that is a correction or is a signal and the tug on the reins that is the rider attempting to catch her balance. In the horse's mind, everything that happens to him while being ridden is a direct reflection on his behavior in that moment. Therefore it is important to identify and prevent unintentional abuse, often caused by poor or inexperienced riding.

Sadly, it is easy to observe harsh, abusive or even cruel treatment of horses at many local shows. Riders feeling the pressure of competition will often yank their horses around with harsh bits, ride with tight tie downs or tense, grabbing legs, force their horses over jumps they are not ready for or inflict various forms of handling that cause pain or confusion. We can see horses over-flexed, jumping with stiff backs or just plain running away with their frustrated riders.

If we were to talk with the majority of these riders, we would discover that not only are they unaware they are hurting their horses, but truly love their horses. Many of the riders sincerely believe their horse is "stubborn," has "issues," is "crazy" or some other label that is commonly used to explain away misunderstood equine behavior. Others simply see so much of this type of treatment, it appears normal to them and they are uninformed as to how it is affecting their horse.

Most of these riders, if not all, would never intentionally mistreat their horses, but their actions feel cruel from the horse's perspective. The horse certainly doesn't understand the difference between intentional cruelty and simple mishandling out of inexperience or ignorance. All the horse knows is he is being hurt, scared or unfairly treated. Therefore it is helpful for riders to distinguish between cruelty and abuse.

Cruelty:

Even persons uneducated about horses can recognize many forms of cruelty such as starving a horse, withholding proper veterinary care, beating the horse out of anger or overworking the horse to the point of exhaustion or lameness. Regrettably, there are many forms of cruelty that are much more subtle. An educated horseman may define cruelty as over-flexing the horse, over-facing the horse, over-bitting the horse or bouncing up and down on his back. Yet if these transgressions are inflicted by an uneducated rider are they cruel?

For this text, we will define cruelty as *intentionally* hurting the horse, or hurting the horse when we know better. For example, the inexperienced rider who jerks the reins is not intentionally being cruel, yet the experienced rider who jerks the reins rather than taking time to train the horse can be judged as cruel.

An educated rider may expand her definition of cruelty to riding below the best of her ability. For example, if, when schooling at the non-interfering level, the rider neglects to use her voice, then kicks the horse, the rider has just punished the horse for no justified reason.

SOME EXAMPLES OF CRUELTY:
- When riding on the non-interfering level, kicking the horse before asking him to move forward by voice

- The rider losing her temper and pulling or jerking on the reins of a frightened or confused horse
- Playing with the horse's mouth, then punishing him for biting
- Riding a lame or exhausted horse
- Asking a horse to perform beyond his physical, mental or emotional abilities

Another, and unfortunately very common, form of cruelty is *lack of consistent and fair* discipline. The educated rider *must* maintain consistent, healthy boundaries for the horse's behavior *at all times*.

It is not fair for the rider to allow the horse to rub his head on her when she is wearing her old stable jacket, then punish him for rubbing when she has on a good show coat. The horse simply doesn't understand the difference.

> **Because the horse will associate anything that happens to him directly to the actions of the rider, it is extremely important that the rider be careful how she is affecting the horse.**

Abuse:

Abuse can often look similar to cruelty and *definitely feels similar* to the horse. The difference is the rider's knowledge and ability.

The horse will associate whatever happens to him to the actions of the rider or handler. For example, in the horse's mind, it is not the ill-fitting saddle that hurts him, it is being mounted by a rider. Because this is how horses associate pain, it is extremely important that the rider be careful how she is affecting the horse.

It is quite common to see riders who "love" their horse, jerking the reins, riding with severe bits, hitting him in the back with an unbalanced seat, asking him to perform beyond his physical ability or inflicting other forms of inappropriate treatment stemming from ignorance. If they knew better, I'm sure the majority of these riders would quickly change their tactics. They are simply uneducated.

Another misconception of many amateur riders who "love" their horse is allowing him to disrespect their space or abuse boundaries. They allow their horse to graze when he is being handled, then become angry when he pulls the reins from their hands trying to graze.

SOME EXAMPLES OF ABUSE:
- A beginner rider pulling on the reins to balance
- A beginner rider gripping with her legs to hold on
- An inexperienced rider bouncing in the saddle
- A rider using a martingale adjusted too tightly without knowing the proper fit
- Riding the horse too hard or long for his current condition without knowing when he is stressed
- Riding the horse over too high jumps or through too high a level of Dressage maneuvers without realizing the horse is not ready.

Unfortunately, the horse does not understand the difference between cruelty and abuse. The only thing a horse knows is he is being hurt. Such inconsistency or lack of boundaries at best is not fun and at worst can make a neurotic or uncontrollable horse.

Since horses were not born with riders on their backs, it is every horseman or woman's responsibility to ride in the least abusive way possible. This can be interpreted as working to increase riding skills and knowledge. Therefore riders unable to ride at advanced levels or who are uninterested in riding at advanced levels can chose to excel on the non-interfering level.

A rider who does not interfere with her horse's natural way of going has accomplished more toward not abusing her horse than the majority of people on horses. Such a rider can also establish that all important and much desired trust between her and the horse, which makes rides infinitely more fun and enjoyable for both herself and her four-legged friend.

> **It is important to identify and prevent unintentional abuse which often results from poor or inexperienced riding.**

As with all forms of energetic communication, these five basic aspects—fairness, leadership, clarity, fun, consistency—are only possible when the horse can "hear" on a level beyond instinctive. A malnourished horse concerned about survival or a horse suffering from pain in his back, hip, shoulder, foot or other sites will not feel he is being fairly treated, will not feel safe with the rider, will not travel at a consistent pace and will certainly not be having fun.

A horse in such a situation is incapable of connecting energetically with the rider through the higher chakras. Chapter 14 discusses signs of malnutrition, pain or fear in horses, which can be easily overlooked or misinterpreted as behavior issues and prevent the horse from moving into this much desired energetic connection.

Part IV

Physical Blocks to Energy Flow

Chapter 14
Hidden First and Second
Chakra Issues

NOTE: *Contents in this chapter are not designed to diagnose or to suggest treatment. It is recommended a qualified equine practitioner be consulted for any questions regarding a horse's health.*

MOST EXPERIENCED HORSEMEN AND WOMEN HAVE HAD the displeasure of riding a horse who is constantly trying to grab bites of grass, won't stand still to be mounted or rushes his jumps. We have all heard inexperienced riders relate stories of horses trying to rub them off on a fence or tree.

Though these types of behavior can be symptoms of poor training or lack of training, they are quite often the result of a horse malnourished or in pain. As we saw with Copper in Chapter 2, a malnourished horse will always be focused on getting the proper nutrition, which is lacking in many of today's over-processed feeds and poor soil. A horse who experiences pain in his back or shoulders from an ill-fitting saddle or a saddle placed too far forward or too far back can be difficult to mount or may rush his fences because he is running away from the pain.

After all, since the rider looks and smells like a carnivore, and all horses know that carnivores are a threat to survival, horses will naturally relate these problems to the rider. Therefore a rider simply cannot gain a horse's trust until basic issues of pain and nutrition have been met.

In addition, since a horse can only focus on one thing at a time, a rider must address the basics of pain and malnutrition before she attempts to bring the horse up into the higher chakras. It is impossible for the horse to trust or cooperate with the rider if his back is sore or his system is screaming at him to eat.

No text on opening and clearing the horse's chakras would be complete without some basic information on how to move a horse out of the survival energy of his first chakra. This can often be achieved by simply addressing some common nutrition and soreness issues.

Nutrition

It is no secret that our society today has a nutrition crisis. Many people, though eating large quantities, are suffering from poor nutrition. In today's world of over-processed foods, we are getting a lot of empty calories, resulting in people who are overweight and poorly nourished.

After a lifetime of studying my personal diet in an attempt to better my own health, I began to look at the diet of my horses. I am not a specialist in the area of equine nutrition, nor am I a vet, but I have noticed that my personal horses are not as focused on food as others seem to be.

My horses will stand next to a bucket of grain without trying to get to it. They will also stand quietly in a grassy field without pulling at the reins to try and graze.

At the same time I have watched other horses dragging their handlers toward any bucket within reach and pulling at the lead rope or reins to graze as soon as they glimpse any grass. What is the difference? Is it all training?

I experimented with turning out several horses, including two of my own, into a field with untouched grass. While the other horses immediately buried their noses in the grass and tore up large mouthfuls, my two horses first investigated the field.

They stood looking around for a moment, then walked the fence line. Finally after checking everything, my two horses selected an area and began to graze.

The difference was my horses had been fed whole grains such as oats, rather than processed food, for years (all his life for one of them). My horses also get an organic vitamin and mineral supplement, which helps them more fully digest and absorb the nutrition from their food. The other horses in the field had always been fed processed feeds such as sweet feed or pellets.

I have come to realize that just as with human food, the more processed the feed, the more empty calories it may contain. This is similar to people eating white bread as opposed to whole grain bread.

Feed dealers make more money selling the processed feeds full of sugars than they make selling whole grains. I have also noticed the horses switched to whole grains eventually seem to be calmer and more attentive to their handlers than those eating the processed feeds.

Nutritional health is directly related to the first chakra. A horse whose system is telling him he needs more nutrition than he is getting in his feed simply cannot ignore that bucket of feed or the rich grass at his feet. Gaining the horse's attention enough to teach him anything becomes a constant battle.

Another concern about a horse who is focused so strongly on food is safety. Such a horse will often become pushy to the point of running a person over to get to the feed. All the discipline in the world is not sufficient to get the horse to listen when his system is forcing him to go after more and more food.

Richard J. Holliday, DVM, Senior Veterinary Consultant, Advanced Biological Concepts Organic Division, who has been actively involved in promoting organic agriculture and holistic veterinary medicine for over forty years said:

> Malnutrition, especially mineral imbalances, will affect the nervous system and brain function of animals. This is especially true of horses. As "prey animals" in the wild, their very survival depended on immediate reactions to any perceived danger. In a training situation, impaired brain function in mineral deficient horses results in individuals that may act dense, flighty and slow to learn.

NOTE: *I have been told by vets that the red trace mineral blocks used by most horse owners are not a good source for quality minerals and can even have adverse affects.*

Regarding the red trace mineral blocks, Holliday said:

> *Minerals in salt-based mineral blocks are not balanced. For example, eating enough to meet the needs of one trace mineral may result in getting too much of another. These imbalances tie up other minerals, thus increasing the problem. Best results are obtained by free choice supplementation of a variety of minerals.*

These are available at Advanced Biological Concepts.

HEALTH

I believe it is fairly obvious that a horse in poor health is not a suitable candidate for any training or riding program. However, there are certain aspects of a horse's health that are not as obvious to the casual observer. For example, to most people, a horse may appear to be quite healthy, but have ulcers or teeth problems. The following are some less obvious health problems often mistaken as behavior or training issues:

TEETH – If a horse has sharp edges on his teeth, he will often resist accepting the bit or will throw his head up when the rider uses the reins. Such a horse may be sore enough in the jaw to be head shy as well.

Rather than having the horse's teeth floated (sharp edges smoothed out), many riders will simply use a tie down. This of course creates problems with the horse's balance and stresses the horse's back and joints.

The horse's teeth should be checked every six months to a year, *regardless of the horse's age,* by a qualified equine dentist.

SORE BACK – If the rider is certain the saddle is fitting properly and she is not abusing the horse's back with her seat, back soreness can be indicative of other problems, such as unbalanced hoof trimming, or a kidney or urinary tract infection. Possible illnesses should be diagnosed by a qualified equine health practitioner.

ILL-FITTING SADDLE – With today's smaller, lighter-weight saddles, the under panels are more narrow and reduce the distribution of weight across the horse's back to a smaller area. In addition, horses today have wider backs than a century ago. Because of these two differences, we are seeing more and more problems related to ill-fitting saddles than have been noticed in the past.

Signs of an ill-fitting saddle include a horse who does not stand quietly for saddling or mounting, tosses his head, pins his ears or even tries to bite when the girth is being tightened.

When ridden, the horse may be short in his shoulder movement or act "cold backed" (as if he wants to buck). Other signs can include stumbling or tripping, not traveling straight, difficulty turning, rushed gaits and carrying the head high.

A wool army blanket is one of the best pads one can use because the wool allows excellent air flow. The blanket can also be folded to somewhat compensate for a saddle that is not a perfect fit. More information can be found in many good texts on saddle fitting.

SADDLE-FITTING BASICS:

- *When the rider is sitting in the saddle, there should be about three fingers' width between the pommel of the saddle and the horse's spine.*
- *The saddle should not interfere with the movement of the horse's shoulder. The point of the stirrup bar should be an inch to two inches behind the edge of the shoulder.*
- *The back of the saddle should not be so long as to interfere with the horse's pelvis—where the back and hindquarters connect. (Many mistake this as the hip.) A good guide is the saddle should not extend past the horse's last rib.*
- *When placed on the horse's back without a blanket, the under part of the saddle should rest smoothly against the horse's back without any gaps.*

ULCERS – Soreness in certain parts of the horse's back can be evidence of ulcers. They can be caused by stress or diet and should be checked by a qualified equine health practitioner.

ARTHRITIS AND JOINT PROBLEMS – Just as with humans, a horse's diet can have a great influence on the health of his joints. As Holliday said, a diet with enough quality minerals will support joint health better than a diet of processed feed and empty calories.

Joint problems can also result from overworking a horse, using an improperly adjusted martingale or working a horse too long in a small circle. Any symptoms of arthritis or joint problems should be diagnosed by a qualified equine health practitioner.

FEET AND SOUNDNESS

Correctly balanced hooves is an important foundation for keeping a horse sound, healthy and pain free. Increasing numbers of horses suffer with hip, shoulder, back and other spine problems that can be directly related to their feet. Simply said: if the horse's feet are not balanced properly, the horse will not be healthy.

Just as with people, a horse suffering from chronic pain may experience a breakdown in his overall health. Symptoms of problems related to unbalanced trimming are varied and often quite subtle. Horses can have sore polls, shoulders, hips, knees, hocks or even teeth problems, simply because one foot is trimmed a bit more on one side than the other.

Imbalanced trimming or shoeing can be compared to a human wearing one shoe with a heel and the other flat. The person's spine will fall out of alignment, and her hips, shoulders and other joints will begin to hurt. The problem would be compounded by adding a weight to that person's back and asking her to balance that weight at speed over uneven terrain and jumps. This is what horses feel when their feet are trimmed or shod unevenly. Just as with people, living for years in pain can eventually compromise a horse's overall health.

A rider can also look at her horse's mane and see potential problems in the horse's feet. Because the muscles in the horse's hindquarters and shoulders connect with the neck, part of the mane may fall to one side or the other if the horse's feet are unbalanced. Knowledgable farriers say the mane near the poll can reflect an imbalance in the hind feet and the mane near the withers can reflect the front feet.

Many of the problems we see today in trimming or shoeing horses are possibly due to the large number of people who are shoeing the horse's feet or hoof capsule instead of addressing the alignment of the whole horse. It takes time for a farrier to watch the horse move, check out how he is balanced and analyze what changes need to be made.

The old saying, "no foot, no horse," is as true today as ever. It is essential that riders research, and be willing to pay enough, to find a qualified farrier. The cost and the time lost in trying to correct problems caused by poor trimming or shoeing is simply not worth the money saved in using a low rate farrier.

> **Hoof problems in horses will trigger the survival instincts in the horse's first chakra.**

Foot problems in horses will directly trigger the survival instincts in the horse's first chakra. A horse who is unbalanced to the point of being sore simply cannot get past the pain to listen and focus on what the rider is asking him to do. Such a horse will never be able to trust his rider because he will immediately relate the pain to the rider.

53. An "upside down" horse's top line (shown here) is underdeveloped and weak because of improper use of muscles. (See text page 240.)

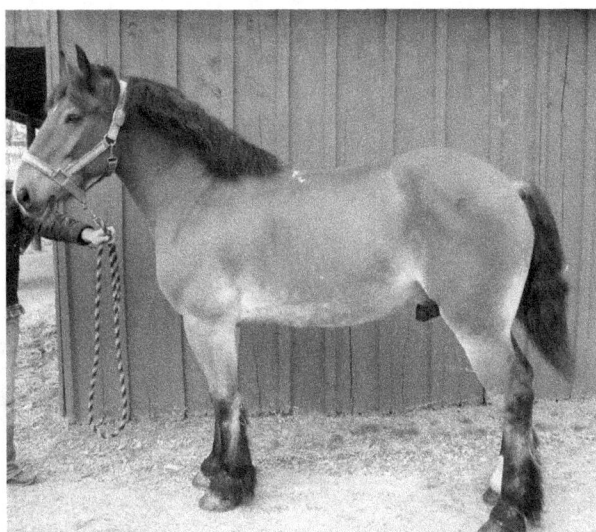

54. A horse whose feet are properly balanced, and who is ridden properly, will have a well developed top line as illustrated by this horse.

Horses with this improper muscle development are often said to be "upside down." Because the horse's legs are not properly supporting his frame, the horse's top line is undeveloped and weak and the hindquarters seem to slant down in the back rather than being well rounded. Some problems related to imbalanced shoeing or trimming are:

HEELS TOO LOW AND UNDER RUN – the angle of the horse's heels is too low. This puts pressure on the heels, causing them to collapse. This is called an under run heel. Low heels usually place the front feet too far out in front of the horse's body and the hind feet too far underneath the body. This prevents the legs from properly supporting the spine and prevents proper muscle development in the back. Often horses that appear to have large bellies with their ribs showing have this problem. Low heels will often cause the horse's sacral joint to drop, producing a "hump" or "bump" at the top of his croup. Low heels usually accompany toes that are too long.

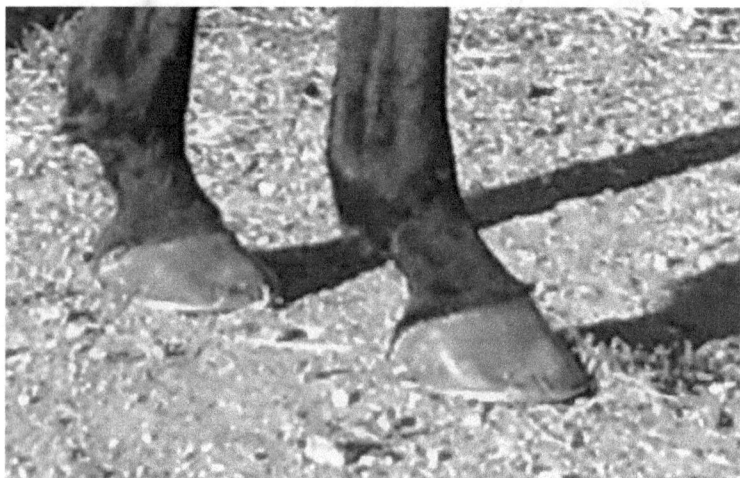

55. When a horse's toes are too long or heels are underrun as shown here, the angle of the hoof is too low, causing soreness in the shoulders, hips and back.

Toes too long – the toes are left too long. The horse sets his toe down first rather than stepping evenly onto the center of the foot. This will affect the arc of the horse's stride and stress his knees, hocks, shoulders, hips and stifles.

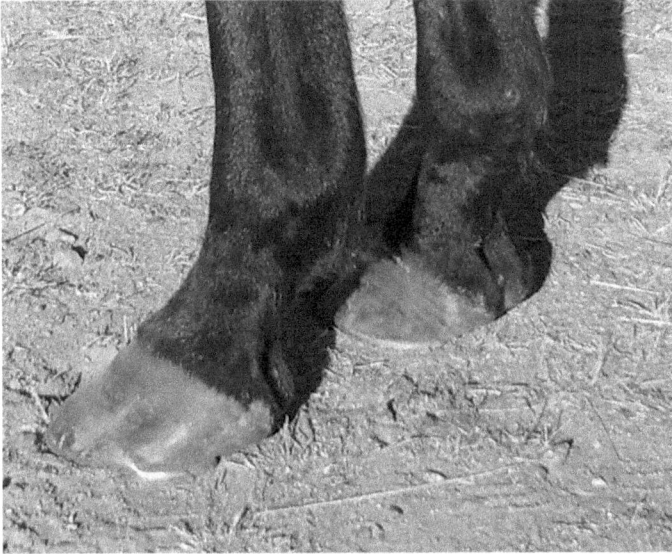

56. If one heel or side of the horse's hoof is trimmed shorter than the other (shown here), the foot will turn in or out.

Toeing in or out – If one heel or side of the horse's hoof is trimmed shorter than the other, the foot will turn in or out, causing the horse's shoulder or hip to drop low on that side. The leg will not move straight forward and the joints are stressed.

Hoof wall weak and crumbly – this is frequently caused by an underrun heel and/or toes too long, which causes pressure on the walls of the hoof and breaks them down. It can also be caused by poor nutrition or wet/dirty conditions.

DROPPED SACRUM – The sacral joint is a triangular bone in the horse's pelvic region. If not properly supported by balanced feet and legs, the bone can shift, causing what appears to be a hump or bump just behind the saddle area. A dropped sacrum can also be a result of improper riding, an accident or riding a horse that is too young. It is difficult for a horse with a dropped sacrum to use the correct muscles in his back and hindquarters, causing the horse to appear "upside down" in his muscle development.

> **The conscious rider looks beyond the obvious and discovers the underlying causes of the horse's behavior.**

As revealed in this chapter, not all horses with a fat belly and a shiny coat are in the best of health. I see so many horses that are mislabeled as "crazy" or "stubborn" simply because they are in pain, unbalanced or are mineral deficient.

It is the conscious rider who looks beyond the obvious and discovers the underlying causes of the horse's behavior. Good nutrition, balanced hoof care, good riding and properly fitted equipment can help many horses overcome acute problems and become present in healthy chakra energy. However, horses stuck in freeze mode or whose energy is blocked by old traumas that they have been unable to release may need more help on both the physical and energetic levels.

Chapter 15 provides information on different alternative modalities that are excellent for clearing old traumas, rebalancing energy patterns and helping the horse become more fully present in his chakras. Once both current issues and old traumas are addressed, the rider will be able to clear and open the horse's chakras and develop a deeper connection with a whole, healthy, happy horse.

Chapter 15
Other Modalities to Support Healthy Energy

FOR THOUSANDS OF YEARS, PEOPLE TREATED THEIR HORSES as investments and cared for them in exchange for a lifetime of service. The horses put food on the table, transported the goods to market and provided the speed needed to escape from enemies. At the least, the loss of a horse could mean harder work and increased poverty. Many times it was the horse that stood between life or death for his owner.

As human life became more mechanized, the importance of the horse as a necessity diminished. People went to work in factories and cities, started buying automobiles and moved away from the farms where horses were essential. Even the farms became automated with big tractors replacing the plow horse.

As a result, horsemanship and knowledge of horses, once part of everyday life, were primarily relegated to those who could afford horses as a pastime and hobby. Growing up with an inherited knowledge of horses became a thing of the past and people began seeking information in books, from those who won ribbons at the local shows and even on the Internet.

Horse ownership transformed into an expensive luxury and trainers started feeling pressured to cut those expenses by producing results more quickly. The old school of knowledge and dedicated training that took a lifetime to learn fell by the wayside as newcomers to the horse world were seduced by quick fixes, "horse whisperers" and marketing hype.

As the demand for faster and faster training methods dovetailed with good marketing, much of the old knowledge became lost. Though a lot of the harsher systems of "breaking" a horse were given up, much of what replaced them is no better. By using kinder-, gentler-sounding words, modern "horse whisperers" continue to stress horses physically, mentally and emotionally, creating a multitude of problems virtually unseen fifty years ago.

So many horses now enter show rings—forced into over flexion and going behind the bit, stressing their necks, backs and lumbosacral joints. Others are overworked in round pens until their hocks and stifles break down. Still others become so stressed from being constantly in freeze mode, it breaks their spirit and adversely affects their digestive health.

Sacred Connections Horsemanship training can make a tremendous difference in the lives of these horses by reducing the stress, taking the pressure off them mentally, physically and emotionally and helping them learn to once again move naturally and feel empowered in their own skin. Unfortunately some horses have been so adversely affected they need more than good riding to bring them back into healthy physical and energetic balance. For these horses some type of alternative healing modality such as massage, acupressure or acupuncture, energy work or structural integration therapy may be of help.

Acupuncture and Acupressure: Acupuncture and acupressure are excellent tools for stimulating the body's healing energies and restoring energy flow to areas that are blocked from trauma or illness. These modalities are commonly used in treating many aliments such as back pain, arthritis, allergies, founder and digestive disorders. Many have successfully used these modalities to improve joint function, help strengthen major organs and improve the overall health of the horse.

Developed by the Chinese more than five thousand years ago, acupuncture and acupressure stimulate the meridian lines of the body. According to ancient Chinese medicine, the meridian lines are energy lines connecting the chakras through which the Chi, or "life force" flows. Areas along the meridian lines, called active points, can be stimulated to induce healing energy to flow through the body.

Acupuncturists use very small, fine needles to stimulate the active points while acupressurists use the fingers to apply pressure or massage to these energetic centers. By stimulating the flow of energy through these points, the body can bring healing energies to vital organs, muscles, bone and other tissues throughout the system.

> Axiatonal therapy works on a cell-deep level to address emotional and spiritual traumas.

Axiatonal Therapy: Whereas acupuncture works to connect with the life force energy on the physical plane, Axiatonal therapy, most commonly administered to humans, works on deep emotional and spiritual levels to connect more directly with Sacred energy. Axiatonal therapy goes cell deep to clear the emotional and spiritual blocks that can interfere with the flow of energy through the chakras.

It is an excellent tool to use with Sacred Connections Horsemanship to help horses release traumas, emotional blocks and other issues that can drain healthy energy and prevent the horse from being fully present in all of his chakras. As with the more familiar acupuncture, Axiatonal therapy is an ancient modality from China, brought to the Western culture in the late 1980s.

Axiatonal therapists use their hands, light and sound to facilitate the flow of energy. This helps bring the patient's spirit back into the present while clearing the meridian lines and chakras.

Results of Axiatonal therapy can be observed in feelings of peace, deep relaxation, resurgence of healthy energy and improved ability to focus. Many people have reported successful use of Axiatonal therapy in pain relief, improved joint function, improved digestion, overall system cleansing, strengthening of major organs and improved general health. I've seen horses who were stiff in their necks, shoulders and backs, become relaxed and start moving much more fluidly after an Axiatonal session.

While administering Axiatonal therapy on horses, I've picked up on old traumas. Owners often react with surprise, exclaiming, "How could you know that?" Once when I received impressions of a horse tangled in a barbed wire fence, the owner exclaimed, "That happened when he was a two-year-old!"

Flushing toxins from the system in a manner of abscesses or fluid draining happens occasionally with energetic therapy. One time I warned an owner that her horse might have some hoof abscesses after the session because he would be cleansing toxins from his system. Sure enough, the next session she described how the horse's entire lower leg had swollen and drained fluid. "I'm glad you warned me," she said. "I would have panicked if I didn't know what it was."

Since Axiatonal therapy works primarily in the energetic system, it is not typically acknowledged by Western medicine. However, like acupuncture, it is an excellent complement to other modalities of healing used in Western medicine. If the body is repaired physically and the energy flow is still out of alignment, then the body may continue to be weak and susceptible to injury or illness.

Massage: Equine massage therapy has gained much popularity in recent years. It is an excellent tool to relieve stiffness and soreness in the horse that may have been caused by overwork, poor riding, an ill-fitting saddle or problems from the horse's past.

Relief of acute muscle pain through massage therapy will support the horse in being able to clear his lower chakras and focus on communication with his rider. The massage therapist can also relieve stiffness throughout the horse's body, allowing for a higher quality of movement and increased ability to respond to the rider's requests.

> Though to the eye they appear similar, massage therapy works on the muscles while rolfing works on the body's facia.

Rolfing Structural Integration: Rolfing releases adhesions in the soft tissue, called fascia, so the body can realign itself and allow a healthy flow of healing energy. It is an excellent treatment for pain caused by ill-fitting saddles, unbalanced hoof trimming, poor riding, dehydration, overwork or injuries.

Adhesions cause shortening of the fascia and can pull joints out of alignment, distorting the body's framework. Gravity then puts pressure on the joints and framework causing pain and discomfort. Especially with horses, if the framework is not supporting the body, it can negatively affect vital organs, such as the digestive system, heart and lungs.

57. Silver's lowered head and relaxed ears demonstrate the release many horses experience through Structural Integration Therapy as performed here by Kelly Snyder of Equine Freedom Solutions

Rolfing has helped me personally recover from many injuries to my spine, including a fractured neck, a cracked sacrum and badly damaged disks. After a series of rolfing sessions, I am pain free and can move much better than I could in years.

My horses have also benefited tremendously from rolfing. I've seen horses release tension in their backs, hips and shoulders and begin to move much more fluidly. I've had horses who are afraid to be mounted because of pain, stand quietly for mounting after rolfing sessions. With the release of pain and tension, horses use their backs properly and develop muscle behind the withers and under the saddle area, changing the horse's top line conformation.

Dr. Ida Rolf originally developed Rolfing in the 1950s for use on humans. In recent years Equine Structural Integration Therapists have had great success in using this modality for horses. Rolfing looks very similar to massage in that the therapist uses his or her hands to work the tissues. However, while massage works on the muscles, Rolfing works on the fascia surrounding the muscles.

Craniosacral Therapy: Craniosacral Therapy focuses on bringing balance throughout the skeletal and muscular systems with specific focus on the individual bones of the skull, spine and sacrum. Rather than focusing on disease or symptoms, the practitioner works with the body's natural rhythms to regenerate a healthy life force. Craniosacral Therapy is increasingly used as a preventive health measure for its ability to bolster resistance to disease and is effective for a wide range of medical problems associated with pain and dysfunction.

Equine Craniosacral therapy can help horses combat the physical stresses and strains imposed on them from poor riding, unbalanced hoof trimming, ill-fitting saddles or overwork. It allows them to rebalance their bodies so they are able to perform more effectively and comfortably over a longer period.

Craniosacral Therapy is an energy-based therapy originally developed for humans by osteopaths in the early 1900s. The therapist uses his or her hands to bring energy to areas of the body in order to release restrictions in its musculoskeletal system and fascia. There is no physical manipulation of bones or tissues, and the body is allowed to readjust at its own pace.

As a therapy it offers an excellent and extremely effective alternative to more conventional therapies such as massage and physiotherapy, especially for nervous and anxious horses. Using a very gentle hands-on approach, craniosacral therapists encourage the horse to release the restricted movement of the bones of the skull, spine and pelvis.

While good veterinary care works primarily with a current state of discomfort, injury or illness, many alternative modalities, such as axiatonal or craniosacral therapies can help clear the energetic connections to past traumas that prevent the horse from becoming healthily present in all his chakras.

For example, a wild horse usually experiences trauma in the form of a physical threat that rarely lasts more than a few moments. He quickly runs away, shakes it off and continues with whatever he was doing.

However, the domesticated horse does not always have that option. He is penned in and cannot escape, and often is prevented—by harsh bits, tie downs, whips, spurs and other equipment—from being able to fight against the trauma. Trauma in domestic horses can last from an hour or more to many years and be repeated on a regular basis.

Unreleased trauma lodges in the cells and prevents a free flow of healthy energy, thus affecting the alignment of the horse's energy patterns. If an energy therapist or body worker (using massage, rolfing or acupressure) can clear this old trauma, it will help open and reconnect the horse's chakras allowing a deeper bond between horse and rider.

It is wise for the horse lover to be cautious in working with her horse's energy. Such work should be done by a certified therapist under the guidance of a licensed veterinarian.

The rider should also be cautioned by the old saying, "A lame horse is a tame horse." If a horse is stuck in freeze mode, is lost in an old trauma or is body sore due to adhesions in his fascia system, he may become quiet, submissive and docile. He may be easy to control regardless of the quality of communication. However, once freed of a state of numbness or freed from soreness or old trauma and with access to a healthy flow of energy, the horse may become much more alive, enthusiastic and present in his body.

> **With good, kind training, horses can become fully engaged and reach their true potential.**

Connecting through the horse's chakra energy is an incredible, spiritual, humbling, life-affirming experience for a rider. It is the free flow of energy between horse and rider of which the poets and bards sing and is the dream of nearly every true horsewoman or man.

However, relating to horses on a deep energetic level is not for everyone. This type of work challenges us to look deeper and more candidly at our horses, ourselves and our riding. Just as with any spiritual practice, some people may not be open to such extraordinary experiences and will not obtain similar results. For others, it is simply not the right time in their lives for this type of work.

Not all riders have the necessary courage to candidly look at their horse and their riding. It is the sincerely dedicated horsewoman who will challenge what she has always believed about "proper" riding. It is the truly courageous rider who will drop the reins and discover how she is actually affecting the horse.

Stephanie was a rider who had the courage to challenge what was happening with her horse. Several years ago a former trainer had pushed Stephanie's beautiful bay Thoroughbred, Johnny, too fast in preparing for the show ring. Johnny was not only refusing his jumps and running away, he refused to load in the trailer to go to shows.

Stephanie stopped riding Johnny altogether and did ground work for a few years. Though this method helped, she wanted more. When Stephanie was ready to begin riding Johnny again, she searched for a trainer who would allow Johnny to work at his own pace.

When I first started working with Stephanie and Johnny, his head was up, he was jumpy, and he wanted to run away at the slightest pretext. Fortunately, Stephanie was willing to start over with lunging and riding on loose reins. She was more than willing to give Johnny a chance to go slowly and build a trusting relationship at his own pace.

Stephanie was also more than willing to end a session when Johnny had done what we asked of him. She understood that to push him for more would only sour him again. She has now become a strong advocate for her horse, always making sure she listens to his input and defends his right to fair treatment.

"He has to have a voice, and I need to defend him," Stephanie said.

Today Stephanie can ride Johnny over jumps and in open fields on a soft snaffle and a loose rein. He no longer bolts and runs away when he is startled and he responds perfectly to a soft voice. Stephanie always seems to be smiling when she rides and often comments on how wonderful he is about not bolting and running.

"He came down just from voice," she often says during our sessions. "That's huge."

Stephanie is hoping to take Johnny back to a show soon, just to help him realize that he will never be pushed or hurt again.

> **Empowering horses through the chakra energy system is not for everybody.**

Stephanie and Johnny are an excellent example of what Sacred Connections Horsemanship is truly about. Johnny was like so many horses that have been "trained." He usually obeyed but never willingly or happily cooperated.

Even with good, kind schooling, the majority of horses are never wholly present or engaged in what they are doing, and most rarely reach their true potential. Though they are successful in their performance, respond well, and their riders can enjoy them, it feels like going through the motions. The horses' hearts and souls are simply not invested in their work.

Most horse lovers today want more than just horses who will submit to their commands. They want their horses to be happy and have as much fun as their riders. Unfortunately what they usually wind up with is domination over their horses rather than full partnerships.

In a desperate search for a happier horse and a more meaningful connection, many horse lovers do their best with one training system after another. Their horses are eventually trained. The horses do what is asked of them, turn when their riders pull the reins, and the horses don't run away and no longer buck.

While this may work perfectly well for some, for others, there is something missing. The spark is not there. Most riders want their horses to do more than just submit to their signals. They want their horses to participate as an equal partner. They want to taste that noble streak of freedom and spirit that made their hearts soar when they first discovered horses.

Sacred Connections Horsemanship is designed for these rare and exceptional horsewomen and men who will challenge themselves to achieve more. It is not for every rider.

The rider who aspires to truly become "one" with such a noble and magnificent being must let go of her fears and be willing to take a deep and honest look at herself and her horse. Such a rider is willing to allow her horse to be all that he is meant to be, not just as she would have him. She must become enlightened enough to be in full partnership with another "whole," enlightened being.

Sacred Connections Horsemanship is not about "how to train your horse." It is about empowering your horse to become a full, whole being in an enlightened partnership with you; another whole being. May your spirits soar together . . .

(

GLOSSARY

Artificial Aids – Tools such as whips or spurs, used to reinforce the natural aids.

Axiatonal Therapy – A technique that uses light and sound on the horse's meridian lines to go cell deep and clear the emotional and spiritual blocks that can interfere with the flow of Sacred energy through the chakras. Axiatonal Therapy originated in China and was introduced in the Western world in the late 1980s.

Behind the bit – A term to describe the horse tucking his nose behind the vertical, avoiding contact with the rider's hands. The horse's jaw and back are usually tense.

Cavaletti – Poles on the ground to maintain even strides. Used primarily in the approach to a jump.

Central balance – The distribution of the horse's weight toward the hindquarters, lightening the forehand. Also called collection.

Chakra – The energy patterns connected to the body's systems, organs and emotional and spiritual structure.

Collection – The distribution of the horse's weight toward the hindquarters, lightening the forehand.

Contact – A continuous feel of the horse's mouth through the reins. The horse's head and neck remain relaxed and stretched forward.

Dynamic balance – The balance of the horse while in motion. The horse's weight shifts from the forehand, through to the hindquarters and back up again, depending on the horse's speed and the terrain.

Engagement of the Hindquarters – Use of the hocks to thrust forward and use of the stifles to pull the hind leg under the body.

Frame – The horse's outline, including his carriage and posture of the head and neck, the engagement of the back and the length and stride of the hind legs.

Flexions – A relaxed retraction of the horse's lower jaw as a result of increased tension on the reins caused by the horse's forward movement in the presence of contact.

Flight, fight or freeze – The states of response prey animals use when threatened.

Impulsion – Energy flowing forward from the hindquarters, signalled for by the rider's legs.

Lateral Agility – The ability of the horse to balance and carry himself and a rider through a turn.

Lunging – An exercise in which the horse moves in circles at the end of a long line that is held by a person. Used for teaching voice commands, stabilization and developing longitudinal agility.

Longitudinal Agility – The ability of the horse to shorten and lengthen his stride.

Natural Aids – Tools such as voice, legs and hands used by the rider to signal the horse.

On the bit – A term used to describe the horse flexing in the jaw, shifting his weight toward his hindquarters, maintaining a forward energy and connecting with the rider's hands through a soft, elastic contact.

Over-flexed – Also called Rollkur or hyperflexion. A state in which the horse's head is behind the vertical and his nose is pulled down and in. Rather than the horse accepting the bit, it dangles in the horse's mouth and his fifth chakra is above his sixth and seventh. Over-flexion usually happens when the horse is taught to flex before he is taught to move forward on the bit or on contact.

Pirouette – Dressage maneuver in which the horse's forehand makes a circle around a smaller circle made by the hindquarters.

Piaffe – A highly collected and cadenced trot in place or nearly in place.

Passage – A highly elevated and powerful trot in which there is a moment of suspension between steps.

Popping a shoulder – The horse evades turning by simply overflexing his neck to the side while continuing in the direction he was already going.

Raised Cavaletti – Poles slightly raised (six inches to a foot) that are used to strengthen horse's back, agility and suspension.

Rollkur – Also called over-flexion or hyperflexion. A state in which the horse's head is behind the vertical and his nose is pulled down and in. Rather than the horse accepting the bit, it dangles in the horse's mouth and his fifth chakra is above his sixth and seventh. Over-flexion usually happens when the horse is taught to flex before he is taught to move forward on the bit or on contact.

Sacred Connections Horsemanship – A combination of classical Forward Riding and classical Dressage along with holistic care for the horse's optimum health and well-being to engage the horse's chakras and connect the horse and rider energetically.

Static balance – Balance of the horse while standing still. Three-fifths of the horse's weight is on the forehand.

Stabilization – The continuous maintenance of even speeds at all gaits, regardless of terrain. The horse continues such a rhythm whether on loose reins or contact, until the rider tells him to change.

Seat/position – The manner in which a rider sits in the saddle.

Semi-collection – Central balance, but with less engagement of the hindquarters and less height in the steps than in full collection. The head remains at the vertical and the horse is through the back.

Through the back – A term used to describe the shifting of the horse's weight toward the hindquarters, and the engagement of the hindquarters. The horse moves energy forward and connects the energy of the third chakra with the fifth. The horse's croup lowers, changing the angle of the sacrum, making it appear that the horse's back lifts just behind the saddle.

Tie down – A standing martingale typically adjusted too tightly, resulting in holding the horse's head down rather than preventing it from rising above the angle of control. Consists of a strap connecting from the horse's girth (cinch) or breast plate to his noseband through the front legs.

Top line – The development of the horse's muscles in the neck, back and hindquarters. A horse is said to have a "good" top line if the line creates a slightly convex effect in the horse's neck and hindquarters.

ACKNOWLEDGMENTS

Training horses and writing are the two passions that have ruled my life. These endeavors have a commonality in that they can both be lonely work.

Therefore, I acknowledge the wonderful humans and incredible equines who kept me company on my journey. I am honored and humbled to count them all good and true friends. These beings have listened and supported, comforted and loved me as I found my voice through these pages. If I have failed to mention one or some other, it is not because my heart does not acknowledge that being—it is because my memory is simply not as strong as my heart.

The horses: Count of War, Swaps' Fair Countes, Fine and Dandy, Me and My Shadow, Warlord, Somewhere's Rainbow, Gypsy Gold, Silver Lining, Sterling Silver and many others.

I would especially like to thank my mother, Gigi Hoelscher, who was my first trainer and who introduced me to Forward Riding when I was too young to understand what a gift it was. I would like to thank my sister, Sharalee Hoelscher, who introduced me to chakra energy work and rolfing. My dad, Vince Hoelscher, for pictures; Kelly Snyder; Marabeth Madson; Meredith MacKenzie; Jeaninie Winborne; Morgan Harrell; Laurel Snyder; Jack Boyd; Ann Fratcher, D.V.M.; Joe Sandven; Brandi Tate; and the many wonderful riders and horse lovers with whom I've had the privilege of working. I would also like to acknowledge Micki Cabaniss Eutsler of Grateful Steps Publishing House for all her hard work and wonderful editing.

A special thanks goes to Jim Helfter, the founder, late owner and CEO of Advanced Biological Concepts, and to Richard J. Holliday, DVM, Senior Veterinary Consultant for Advanced Biological Concepts, www.abcplus.biz.

SELECTED REFERENCES

Harris, Susan E. *Horse Gaits, Balance and Movement.* Hoboken, N.J.: Wiley Publishing, Inc., 1993.

Littauer, Vladimir S. *Common Sense Horsemanship.* New York, N. Y.: D. Van Nostrand Company, Inc., 1951

Cronin, Paul D. *Schooling and Riding the Sport Horse.* Charlottesville, V.A. University of Virginia Press, 2004.

Levine, Peter A., Ph.D. *Waking the Tiger: Healing Trauma.* Berkeley, CA, North Atlantic Books, 1997.

Myss, Caroline. *Anatomy of the Spirit: The Seven Stages of Power and Healing.* New York, N.Y. Three Rivers Press, 1996.

Dillon, Jane Marshall. *School for Young Riders.* New York, N. Y. : Arco Publishing, 1973

Heuschmann, Gerd, D.V.M. *Tug of War: Classical versus "Modern" Dressage.* North Pomfret, Vermont: Trafalgar Square Books, 2007

INDEX

ABOUT THE AUTHOR

Catherine Hunter has worked with horses for more than fifty-five years and is a nationally rated rider/instructor, a licensed trainer and former police horse trainer. She is The Peace Rider, who rode her Thoroughbred, Count of War, nine hundred miles from South Carolina to Ground Zero in New York City.

Catherine's more than forty years of professional equine experience includes developing and teaching an equine-based curriculum for technical schools and colleges. She has served as equine consultant and wrangler for feature films, worked as host and consultant for equine-related cable TV shows and judged horse shows throughout the Southeastern U.S.

Catherine's instructors include former Olympic riders and coaches, ANRC National Judges, U.S. Cavalry Instructors and nationally acclaimed authors. She has also studied with international equine osteopaths, craniosacral therapists and leading farriers. Catherine is a certified Axiatonal Therapist and is a pioneer in the field of Equine Energetics.

As an award-winning journalist, Catherine has published in national and regional equine publications, such as *The Chronicle of The Horse*, *The Western Horse* and *John Lyons' Perfect Horse Magazine*.

Catherine was a recognized member of the Mooreland Fox Hunt for more than twenty-five years, served as a huntsman for the Royal Meridian St. Leonard's Day Hunt and served as a professional Whipper In for the Early Grove Hounds. She has taught riding clinics throughout the Eastern U.S. for pony clubs, 4H and other equine-affiliated organizations.

As an historical cavalry reenactor for twenty years, Catherine has served as staff courier and mounted security for the largest reenactments in history and has been a keynote speaker for national and regional events.

For information on the author's clinics, retreats and speaking engagements, contact <u>sacredconnectionshorsemanship.com</u>.

www.ingramcontent.com/pod-product-compliance
Lightning Source LLC
Chambersburg PA
CBHW062204270326
41930CB00009B/1646